CliffsNotes™

The Things They Carried

By Jill Colella

IN THIS BOOK

- Learn about the life and background of Tim O'Brien

- Preview an introduction to *The Things They Carried*

- Explore the novel's themes and character development in the Critical Commentaries

- Examine in-depth Character Analyses

- Acquire an understanding of the novel with Critical Essays

- Reinforce what you learn with CliffsNotes Review

- Find additional information to further your study in the Cliffs-Notes Resource Center and online at www.cliffsnotes.com

Houghton Mifflin Harcourt
Boston   New York

About the Author

Jill Colella earned a master's degree at the University of Maryland in English literature, specializing in Vietnam War narratives in film and literature. Ms. Colella, the daughter of a Vietnam veteran, founded The Children of Vietnam Combat Veterans Project in 1997 to speak to the specific concerns of families of veterans. She is the author of *After Vietnam: War Stories from a Veteran's Daughter*, a memoir of the effects her father's service in Vietnam had on her family life.

Publisher's Acknowledgments
Editorial

Project Editor: Michael Kelly

Acquisitions Editor: Gregory W. Tubach

Glossary Editors: The editors and staff at Webster's New World™ Dictionaries

Editorial Administrator: Michelle Hacker

Composition

Indexer: York Production Services, Inc.

Proofreader: York Production Services, Inc.

Wiley Indianapolis Composition Services

CliffsNotes™ *The Things They Carried*

Copyright © 2001 Houghton Mifflin Harcourt

Library of Congress Control Number: 00-107702

ISBN: 0-7645-8668-8

Printed in the United States of America

DOC 10 9 8 7 6

4500477969

1O/RU/RR/QV/IN

For information about permission to reproduce selections from this book, please write Permissions, Houghton Mifflin Harcourt Publishing Company, 215 Park Avenue South NY NY 10003.

www.hmhco.com

Table of Contents

Life and Background of the Author 1

  Personal Background 2
      The Early Years 2
      Education and Vietnam 3
  Career Highlights... 4
      Reconciliation through Storytelling........................ 4
      Major Works... 5

Introduction to the Novel 9

  Introduction... 10
  A Brief Synopsis... 13
  List of Characters... 15
  Character Map.. 20

Critical Commentaries 21

  The Things They Carried.. 22
  Love... 27
  Spin... 29
  On the Rainy River 32
  Enemies/Friends.. 38
  How to Tell a True War Story................................... 42
  The Dentist 46
  Sweetheart of Song Tra Bong 49
  Stockings 53
  Church... 55
  The Man I Killed/Ambush.. 57
  Style.. 61
  Speaking of Courage 63
  Notes 67
  In the Field... 70
  Good Form 73
  Field Trip 75
  The Ghost Soldiers... 77
  Night Life 82
  The Lives of the Dead 84

Character Analyses. 87
  "Tim O'Brien" 88
  Lt. Jimmy Cross 89
  Norman Bowker. 90
  Mary Anne Bell 91
  Kiowa. 92
  Rat Kiley 92
  Linda 93
  Henry Dobbins 94

Critical Essays. 95
  The Things They Carried in a Historical Context. 96
  Narrative Structure in *The Things They Carried* 97
  Style and Storytelling in *The Things They Carried*. 98
  The Things They Carried and Loss of Innocence 99
  The Things They Carried and Questions of Genre 101

CliffsNotes Review 103
  Fill in the Blank 103
  Identify the Quote 104
  Essay Questions 106
  Practice Projects 107

CliffsNotes Resource Center 108
  Books. 108
    Primary Sources 108
    Secondary Sources. 108
    Articles 109
  Film. 110
  Internet Resources 110
  Send Us Your Favorite Tips. 111

Appendix: Map of Vietnam. 112

Index. 113

How to Use This Book

This CliffsNotes study guide on O'Brien's *The Things They Carried* sup-plements the original literary work, giving you background information about the author, an introduction to the work, a graphical character map, critical commentaries, expanded glossaries, and a comprehensive index, all for you to use as an educational tool that will allow you to better understand *The Things They Carried*. This study guide was written with the assumption that you have read *The Things They Carried*. Reading a literary work doesn't mean that you immediately grasp the major themes and devices used by the author; this study guide will help supplement your reading to be sure you get all you can from O'Brien's *The Things They Carried*. CliffsNotes Review tests your comprehension of the original text and reinforces learning with questions and answers, practice projects, and more. For further information on Tim O'Brien and *The Things They Carried*, check out the CliffsNotes Resource Center.

CliffsNotes provides the following icons to highlight essential elements of particular interest:

Reveals the underlying themes in the work.

Helps you to more easily relate to or discover the depth of a character.

Uncovers elements such as setting, atmosphere, mystery, passion, violence, irony, symbolism, tragedy, foreshadowing, and satire.

Enables you to appreciate the nuances of words and phrases.

Don't Miss Our Web Site

Discover classic literature as well as modern-day treasures by visiting the Cliffs-Notes Web site at www.cliffsnotes.com. You can obtain a quick download of a CliffsNotes title, purchase a title in print form, browse our catalog, or view online samples.

You'll also find interactive tools that are fun and informative, links to interesting Web sites, tips, articles, and additional resources to help you, not only for literature, but for test prep, finance, careers, computers, and the Internet too. See you at www.cliffsnotes.com!

LIFE AND BACKGROUND OF THE AUTHOR

The following abbreviated biography of Tim O'Brien is provided so that you might become more familiar with his life and the historical times that possibly influenced his writing. Read this Life and Background of the Author section and recall it when reading O'Brien's *The Things They Carried*, thinking of any thematic relationship between O'Brien's work and his life.

Personal Background **2**

Career Highlights **4**

Personal Background

The author Tim O'Brien is not unlike the character called "Tim" that he created for his novel, *The Things They Carried*, as both author and character carry the stories of similarly experienced lives. O'Brien not only shares the same name as his protagonist but also a similar biographical background. Readers should note and remember that although the actual and fictional O'Briens have some experiences in common, *The Things They Carried* is a work of fiction and not a non-fiction autobiography. This distinction is key and central to understanding the novel.

The Early Years

Like "O'Brien," Tim O'Brien, born William Timothy O'Brien, Jr., spent his early life first in Austin, Minnesota, and later in Worthington, Minnesota, a small, insulated community near the borders of Iowa and South Dakota. The first of three children, O'Brien was born on October 1, 1946, at the beginning of the post-World War II baby boom era.

His childhood was an American childhood. O'Brien's hometown is small-town, Midwestern America, a town that once billed itself as "the turkey capital of the world," exactly the sort of odd and telling detail that appears in O'Brien's work. Worthington had a large influence on O'Brien's imagination and early development as an author: O'Brien describes himself as an avid reader when he was a child. And like his other main childhood interest, magic tricks, books were a form of bending reality and escaping it. O'Brien's parents were reading enthusiasts, his father on the local library board and his mother a second grade teacher.

O'Brien's childhood is much like that of his characters—marked by an all-American kid-ness, summers spent on little league baseball teams and, later, on jobs and meeting girls. Eventually, the national quiescence and contentment of the 1950s gave way to the political awareness and turbulence of the 1960s, and as the all-American baby boom generation reached the end of adolescence, they faced the reality of military engagement in Vietnam and a growing divisiveness over war at home.

Education and Vietnam

O'Brien was drafted for military service in 1968, two weeks after completing his undergraduate degree at Macalester College in St. Paul, Minnesota, where he had enrolled in 1964. He earned a bachelor's degree in government and politics. An excellent student, O'Brien looked forward to attending graduate school and studying political science. During the course of his college career, O'Brien came to oppose the war, not as a radical activist but as a campaign supporter and volunteer of Eugene McCarthy, a candidate in the 1968 presidential election who was openly against the Vietnam War.

In 1968, the war in Vietnam reached its bloodiest point in terms of American casualties, and the government relied on conscription to recruit more soldiers. Further, graduate school deferments, which exempted students from the draft, were beginning to be discontinued, though O'Brien did not seek out this recourse. Disappointed and worried, O'Brien—like his character "Tim O'Brien"—spent the summer after his graduation working in a meatpacking plant. Unlike his character, however, O'Brien passed his nights pouring out his anxiety and grief onto the typewritten page. He believes it was this experience that sowed the seeds for his later writing career: "I went to my room in the basement and started pounding the typewriter. I did it all summer. My conscience kept telling me not to go, but my whole upbringing told me I had to."

O'Brien hated the war and thought it was wrong, and he often thought about fleeing to Canada. Unlike his fictional alter ego, however, he did not attempt it. Instead, O'Brien yielded to what he has described as a pressure from his community to let go of his convictions against the war and to participate—not only because he had to but also because it was his patriotic duty, a sentiment that he had learned from his community and parents who met in the Navy during World War II. "It's not Worthington I object to, it's the kind of place it is," O'Brien told an interviewer. "The not knowing anything and not tolerating any dissent, that's what gets to me. These people sent me to Vietnam, and they didn't know the first thing about it."

O'Brien ultimately answered the call of the draft on August 14, 1968 and was sent to Army basic training at Fort Lewis, Washington. He was later assigned to advanced individual training and soon found himself in Vietnam, assigned to Firebase LZ Gator, south of Chu Lai. (The appendix of this book includes a map of Vietnam, including areas referred to in the novel.) O'Brien served a 13-month tour in-country from 1969 to 1970 with Alpha Company, the Fifth Battalion of the 46th Infantry, 198th Infantry Brigade, Americal Division. He was a regular foot soldier, or, as commonly referred to in veterans' slang, a "grunt," serving in such roles as rifleman and radio telephone operator (RTO). He was wounded twice while in service and was relatively safe during the final months of his tour when he was assigned to jobs in the rear. O'Brien ultimately rose to the rank of sergeant.

After returning from his tour in March 1970, O'Brien resumed his schooling and began graduate work in government and political science at Harvard University, where he stayed for nearly five years but did not complete a dissertation.

Career Highlights

In May 1974, O'Brien went to work briefly for *The Washington Post* as a national affairs reporter before his attention was fully diverted to the craft of fiction writing. He began and continues to publish regularly in various periodicals, including *The New Yorker, The Atlantic Monthly, Harper's, Esquire,* and *Playboy,* frequently excerpting parts of his novels as autonomous short stories.

Reconciliation through Storytelling

Of particular note is a piece O'Brien wrote for *The New York Times Magazine* about returning to Vietnam—his first trip back since his service there. In "The Vietnam in Me," O'Brien probes the intersection between memory, time, and witnessing the Vietnam War and his personal relationships. Usually guarded and self-conscious as a public subject—for example, it is rare to find a photo of O'Brien without his signature baseball cap—his article was intimate and highly personal. O'Brien made the trip back to Vietnam with a woman for whom he left his wife, and he makes this plain in the article. O'Brien also addresses other sensitive and personal subjects such as his own readjustment after serving in Vietnam: "Last night," he wrote, "suicide was on my mind. Not whether, but how."

Despite his personal difficulties and despite his intention to cease writing after completing *In the Lake of the Woods* (1994), O'Brien continues to produce works that illuminate the human response to war and articulate the strain associated with veterans (like O'Brien himself) reconciling what they saw and did during the Vietnam War with the values and mores they had learned prior to Vietnam.

O'Brien maintains that *The Things They Carried* "is meant to be about man's yearning for peace. At least [he] hopes it is taken that way." For O'Brien, through his own writing career and through the veteran characters he has conceived, this "yearning" is partially satisfied through the act of storytelling, getting at the truth of an idea or event by retelling and embellishing it. In this way, *The Things They Carried* is a culmination of O'Brien's earlier works and is a culmination of themes—courage, duty, memory, guilt, and storytelling—present in all his works.

Major Works

O'Brien's first published work was a war memoir and account of his year as a "grunt" in Vietnam, *If I Die in a Combat Zone: Box Me Up and Ship Me Home* (1973). This book begins probing the themes that dominate most of O'Brien's works, particularly the issue of moral courage. He followed up his autobiographical account with a debut novel entitled *Northern Lights* (1975), which posits two brothers against one another as foils—one brother went to Vietnam and the other did not. The crux of the novel, which is set in O'Brien's native Minnesota, is a cruel blizzard against which both brothers must struggle. Through this experience, the brothers learn more about each other, and their own motivations and values are illuminated in their own minds. This early work signals the reflection, self-reference, and thorough interior probing of characters that will become the hallmark of O'Brien's style.

O'Brien's next novel departs from the more traditional form of *Northern Lights*. *Going After Cacciato* (1978) is a more surreal and fantastical novel that brought O'Brien to wider public acclaim and earned him the 1979 National Book Award in fiction. A sort of dark, ironic comedy, the subject, an Army private, Cacciato, who catalyzes the story's action, deserts his unit in Vietnam and heads for the Paris peace talks. Literally walking away from the war, the other members of his unit are ordered to pursue him. The story is told from the point of view of Paul Berlin, the character that most resembles O'Brien, as they follow Cacciato across the world. O'Brien begins to push the limits of truth and believability in this novel as well as the bounds of temporality, both stylistic choices that reappear in *The Things They Carried*.

Nuclear Age (1985) was O'Brien's third novel and the farthest departure from his own experience. Set in 1995, O'Brien's protagonist, William Cowling, is a middle-aged man who grew up under the atomic umbrella, so to speak. He suffers severe paranoia over the possibility of nuclear war and finds solace in digging a hole in his backyard as an attempt to bury and quiet all the thoughts that antagonize him. Again, in this novel, O'Brien demonstrates his adeptness in creating a comic look at serious subjects, this being the real fear and threat of the Bomb.

After a two-year interim, O'Brien's short story, "The Things They Carried," the first vignette in the later novel of the same name, was first published in Esquire, and it received the 1987 National Magazine Award in Fiction. The short story was also selected for the *1987 Best American Short Stories* volume and for inclusion in the *Best American Short Stories of the 1980s*. Additionally, O'Brien's short stories have been anthologized in *The O. Henry Prize Stories* (1976, 1978, 1982), *Great Esquire Fiction, Best American Short Stories,* (1977, 1987), *The Pushcart Prize* (Volumes II and X), and in many textbooks and Vietnam-related collections.

O'Brien published *The Things They Carried* in 1990, returning to the immediate setting of Vietnam during the war, which is present in his other novels. O'Brien's return to the rich raw materials of his own experience proved fruitful, as *The Things They Carried* won the 1990 *Chicago Tribune* Heartland Award in fiction. The novel was selected by *The New York Times* as one of the year's ten best novels and was a finalist for a Pulitzer Prize. In 1991, O'Brien was awarded the Melcher Award for *The Things They Carried* and won France's Prix du Meilleur Livre Etranger in 1992.

The follow-up novel, *In the Lake of the Woods,* published in 1994, again takes up the major themes seen in O'Brien's work: guilt, complicity, culpability, and moral courage. O'Brien invents protagonist John Wade, a Vietnam veteran who aspires to win a senatorial election. He loses by a landslide, however, as charges about his complicity in the My Lai massacre come to light during his campaign. To recover from the defeat, John and his wife Kathy stay at a cabin on the shores of a Minnesota lake. O'Brien couches the novel in the style of magical realism and adds an element of mystery as Kathy disappears, and blame for her disappearance (and possible death) fall on her husband. John is forced to confront the deep denial he harbors about his participation in the war as O'Brien raises larger questions about the fallout of war and the consequences of wars after the fighting has ceased and the participants return home changed. *In the Lake of the Woods* won the James Fenimore Cooper Prize from the Society of American Historians and was selected as the best novel of 1994 by *Time* magazine.

In his most recent novel, *Tomcat in Love,* O'Brien creates a Vietnam veteran protagonist, Tom Chippering, though the subject of O'Brien's novel is not war, but love. A *New York Times* Notable Book of the Year, *Tomcat in Love* is a comic novel about a sexist, politically incorrect hero, one that readers love to hate. O'Brien explains that [his] "real fans will love the book. There are so-called fans who are basically Vietnam junkies, but the people who appreciate the writing will like this. I think this is my best book."

O'Brien has received awards from the Guggenheim Foundation, the National Endowment for the Arts, and the Massachusetts Arts and Humanities Foundation. Adept at sly comic fiction about mundane or serious topics, O'Brien is a master of creative storytelling, a manipulator of literary form, and one of the most challenging authors of his time in terms of how he intermixes form and content.

INTRODUCTION TO THE NOVEL

The following Introduction section is provided solely as an educational tool and is not meant to replace the experience of your reading the work. Read the Introduction and A Brief Synopsis to enhance your understanding of the work and to prepare yourself for the critical thinking that should take place whenever you read any work of fiction or nonfiction. Keep the List of Characters and Character Map at hand so that as you read the original literary work, if you encounter a character about whom you're uncertain, you can refer to the List of Characters and Character Map to refresh your memory.

Introduction. 10

A Brief Synopsis 13

List of Characters 15

Character Map 20

Introduction

   The Things They Carried is a powerful meditation on the experiences of foot soldiers in Vietnam and after the war. The work is simultaneously a war autobiography, writer's memoir, and group of fictional short stories. Subtitled "A Work of Fiction," O'Brien immediately and deliberately blurs the line between fact and fiction by dedicating the novel to individuals that the reader soon discovers are the novel's fictional characters. To further complicate the genre blending and blurring between fiction and reality, O'Brien creates a protagonist, a Vietnam veteran, named "Tim O'Brien." The creation of this fictional persona allows O'Brien to explore his real emotions as though they were fictional creations, and simultaneously challenges us when we dismiss a story as fiction when it could just as easily be true. The originality and innovation of O'Brien's invented form are what make the novel particularly compelling because its main theme—more so than even the Vietnam War—is the act of storytelling. Storytelling becomes an expression of memory and a catharsis of the past. Many characters in the novel seek resolution of some kind.

   Readers should note the designations used in this study guide to distinguish between the author, Tim O'Brien, and the fictionalized character, "Tim O'Brien," who is the main character of the novel. While O'Brien and "O'Brien" share a number of similarities, readers should remember that the work is a novel and not an autobiography of the writer who wrote it. Instead, the novel is presented as the autobiography of the fictional character.

   The medium becomes part of the novel's message; the unreliable protagonist "Tim O'Brien" continually questions the veracity of the stories he tells and the hearsay he retells, causing, in turn, the readers to question the veracity of the very stories that O'Brien confronts them with. For example, at one point we believe O'Brien, such as when he describes his fear and shock after killing a Vietnamese soldier, but he then challenges us by casting doubt on the soldier's life and existence. The act of storytelling becomes more important than the stories told. This quality is a characteristic of many fiction and non-fiction works that comprise the Vietnam War literature genre.

   The Vietnam War era was a historical moment marked by confusion and conflict, from the disagreement over the war to the inconsistent and unstructured war of attrition that soldiers were asked to fight. This confusion and conflict is often experienced by individuals in

Vietnam War literature as well, a sort of microcosm of the larger macro-cosm of disorder and chaos. This theme of chaos leads to the tone of uncertainty present in *The Things They Carried*. For example, O'Brien describes how "Tim O'Brien" struggles to decide whether he should avoid military service by fleeing to Canada. The historical issue of draft-dodging, that is, escaping from the country to avoid the military draft, was a high pressure topic about which many contemporary organiza-tions felt strongly. O'Brien takes us through both sides of the issue, feel-ing the fear of a young man facing military service and possibly death to one feeling a patriotic duty toward his country. Many of O'Brien's stories in *The Things They Carried* highlight important historical ten-sions regarding Vietnam and present multiple perspectives, leaving the reader with more questions than answers.

One of the important themes O'Brien confronts in the novel is the pressure caused by feeling the need to adhere to some cultural or com-munity standard of duty, courage, or patriotism. Commonly referred to as "jingoism," this notion is a frequent theme in Vietnam War related fiction, as most soldiers who fought in Vietnam were born and reared just after World War II. (Soldiers in World War II are thought of as hav-ing a much less conflicted sense of their place in the war and their duty to their country, although it was by no means without debate.) Soldiers in Vietnam, therefore, absorbed the mores and values of their parent's generation—that is, the so-called G.I. generation who fought World War II—including duty, patriotism, and service.

Many young men who enlisted or were drafted found, once in Viet-nam, that what they saw there and what they did there contradicted the message of service they had absorbed as they grew into their political consciousness during the Kennedy administration and the continued expansion of the Cold War. These feelings of confusion were fueled in large part by social action in the U.S., including peace rallies, the Hip-pie movement, and resistance music of the 60s and 70s. Prominent examples of this growing pressure are the Woodstock Music Festival in 1969, a gathering of music and people that supported peace and opposed war, and the violent anti-war protests at the Democratic National Convention in Chicago in 1968.

Even at its time, the U.S. involvement in the Vietnam War brought on strong debates for and against, from within the War community and from without. O'Brien inserts himself and his characters into this dis-cussion, using pressing images such as a young Vietnamese girl danc-ing in the midst of rubble and corpses, as well as the character of Henry

Dobbins who, although an effective soldier, harbors thoughts of joining the clergy. O'Brien gives his readers the opportunity to take sides on many of these debates, but always reminds readers that their thoughts are products more of themselves than any intrinsic meaning in the stories of war.

O'Brien demonstrates this—the reminder that what we think is a product of our own perceptions and recollections—through his innovative form. He sets out deliberately to manipulate the audience as they read his work, an act intended to provoke his audience into forming an opinion not about the Vietnam War, but about storytelling (or more precisely, story hearing). For example, O'Brien sets his reader up for a confirmation as he sketches out "Speaking of Courage," a seemingly traditional narrative about a soldier's difficulty readjusting to civilian life. O'Brien uses a narrative style called *free indirect discourse,* where the narrator supplies necessary information about Norman Bowker, and readers have no reason to doubt this information.

But, in the next chapter, "Notes," O'Brien invites his readers into his writing studio, so to speak, by describing how the story of Norman Bowker came to be written. In doing so, "O'Brien" explains that some of the information he provided in "Speaking of Courage" was true and some was invented. By pointing out this inconsistency of factual truth, "O'Brien"/O'Brien challenges readers to make judgments about how much they value storytelling and why they value it. For example, do readers need a story to be actual and factual to believe it? Is a story that is fantastical (such as "The Sweetheart of Song Tra Bong") valuable? Should it be believed? O'Brien's choice of form raises a fact or fiction debate and also answers it: Any distinction between fact and fiction is a moot point.

For O'Brien, the "factuality" or "fictionality" of a story is, by far, secondary to the effect of the story on the reader. If the work evokes an emotional response, then it is a truth. For "O'Brien"/O'Brien, the primacy of emotion is a metaphorical comment on war: "In war you lose your sense of the definite, hence your sense of truth itself, and therefore it's safe to say that in a true war story, nothing is ever absolutely true." O'Brien's form, an amalgamation of the choices to share his protagonist's name, to write a series of related vignettes, and the deliberate blurring of the boundary between fact and fiction, is meant to create a loss of the "sense of the definite" in the reader. Literary critic Toby Herzog suggests that "the ambiguity and complexity of the book's form and content also mirror for readers the experience of war."

While part of O'Brien's objective is to create an aesthetic that simulates the chaos and uncertainty that characterized soldiers' experiences, within the genre of War literature, specifically Vietnam War-related Literature, O'Brien's novel does the opposite. *The Things They Carried,* with its stylistic ambiguity, is also a tool for understanding the Vietnam War. Literature has often been used as a path to understanding history, and O'Brien follows the tradition of literary precursors such as Wilfred Owen, Ernest Hemingway, and Graham Greene.

O'Brien's novel originates at an important post-war moment, one which differed greatly from the post-World War I era in which Hemingway wrote. The main differences and obstacles for Vietnam veterans were the divisiveness of the war and the tide of public opinion opposing the war. Vietnam veterans' return from the war—unlike the return of soldiers from World War I and World War II—was not celebrated or lauded. As the Nixon administration transitioned to the Ford administration, the general public wanted to forget about the longest foreign military involvement by the U.S. and the failure of this engagement to bring about its intended agenda. In short, the United States had not clearly won or lost, and the esteem of veterans suffered. Throughout the late 70s and early 80s, veterans struggled to receive recognition and to bring attention to the problems of post-traumatic stress disorder and survivor guilt from which many veterans suffered. Vietnam veterans such as Tim O'Brien, John Delvecchio, and Al Santoli helped to spark and maintain interest in a public discourse on the war.

The ambiguity of *The Things They Carried* reflects the lack of resolution of the war and illuminates the necessity to use fact, fiction, or fictionalized fact to tell the stories of Vietnam.

A Brief Synopsis

Called both a novel and a collection of interrelated short stories, Tim O'Brien's *The Things They Carried* is a unique and challenging book that emerges from a complex variety of literary traditions. O'Brien presents to his readers both a war memoir and a writer's autobiography, and complicates this presentation by creating a fictional protagonist who shares his name. To fully comprehend and appreciate the novel, particularly the passages that gloss the nature of writing and storytelling, it is important to remember that the work is fictional rather than a conventional non-fiction, historical account.

Protagonist "Tim O'Brien" is a middle-aged writer and Vietnam War veteran. The primary action of the novel is "O'Brien's" remembering the past and working and reworking the details of these memories of his service in Vietnam into meaning.

Through a series of linked semi-autobiographical stories, "O'Brien" illuminates the characters of the men with whom he served and draws meaning about the war from meditations on their relationships. He describes Lt. Jimmy Cross as an inexperienced and ill-equipped leader of Alpha Company, both in-country and at a post-war reunion. Years after the war, the two spent an afternoon together remembering their friends and those who were killed.

In the introductory vignette, O'Brien describes each of the major characters by describing what they carry, from physical items such as canteens and grenades and lice to the emotions of fear and love that they carry. After the first chapter, the narrator is identified as "Tim O'Brien," a middle-aged writer and veteran.

"O'Brien" relates personal stories, among them a story that he had never divulged before about how he planned to flee to Canada to avoid the draft. "O'Brien," who spent the summer before he had to report to the Army working in a meatpacking factory, left work early one day and drove toward Canada, stopping at a fishing lodge to rest and devise a plan. He is taken in by the lodge owner, who helps him confront the issue of evading the draft by taking him out on the lake that borders Canada. Ultimately, "O'Brien" yields to what he perceives as societal pressures to conform to notions of duty, courage, and obligation, and he returns home instead of continuing on to Canada. Through the telling of this story, "O'Brien" confesses what he considers a failure of his convictions: He was a coward because he went to participate in a war in which he did not believe.

As a writer, O'Brien constantly analyzes and comments upon how stories are told and why they are told. For example, he tells the story of Curt Lemon's death and proceeds to analyze and explain why it holds an element of truth. Ultimately, he surmises, "truth in a story is not necessarily due to 'factual' accuracy." Instead, if the story affects the reader or listener in a personal and meaningful way, then that emotion is the truth of the story. O'Brien tests these ideas by relating the stories that others told in Vietnam, like the story of a soldier who brought his girlfriend to Vietnam and grows more and more terrified as she becomes fascinated by the war and ultimately never returns home. The soldiers who hear the story doubt its truth, but are drawn into the story nonetheless, showing that factual accuracy is less important to truth than emotional involvement.

The recurring memory of the novel that O'Brien recalls as a sort of coda, or repeated image, is the death of his friend and fellow soldier, Kiowa. Kiowa was a soft-spoken Native American with whom "O'Brien" made a strong connection. The scene of Kiowa's death in a battlefield becomes the basis for several of the novel's vignettes: "Speaking of Courage," "In the Field," "Field Trip," and "Notes." In each of these, O'Brien recalls snippets of memory and builds an indictment against the wastefulness of the war.

In "Speaking of Courage," the fictional "O'Brien" presents a story that he wrote about a Vietnam comrade named Norman Bowker. "O'Brien" describes Bowker's difficulty adjusting to civilian life after he returns from Vietnam as he recalls his own ease slipping back into the routine of daily life, which for him was graduate school. In the end, in "Notes," "O'Brien" describes how Bowker suggested that he ("O'Brien") write a story about a veteran with problems readjusting and intense feelings of survivor guilt. "O'Brien" realizes that he must not have put the memories of Vietnam behind him because he constantly writes about them.

Finally, "O'Brien" remembers a girl from his childhood who died from cancer, the first dead body he saw before being in-country. He describes how as a little boy, "Timmy," he could dream her alive and see and talk to her. He recognizes the similarity of his ability to animate her in his mind and his writing about Vietnam, and realizes that he tells these stories to save his own life.

List of Characters

"Tim O'Brien"   The protagonist of the novel, "O'Brien" symbolizes memory and storytelling, two central themes of the novel. He is a young foot soldier in the Vietnam War, a member of Alpha Company. He is also the fictional persona of O'Brien the writer, and similarly is a middle-aged writer with a Midwestern, middle-class

background that informs his values. Readers follow "O'Brien"
around Vietnam, experiencing his fear, guilt, curiosity, and blood
lust. For all of the first hand accounts and stories, "O'Brien" is the
readers' source, and he demonstrates the danger of believing that
something is either fact or fiction, often by evoking emotions in
the reader.

Kiowa Kiowa symbolizes the wastefulness of war. He is a foot soldier in Alpha Company, a Native American Baptist who always
keeps an illustrated New Testament with him. He is O'Brien's clos-
est friend in Vietnam and is killed in battle when he drowns in a
field during a flood. When "O'Brien" returns to Vietnam, he visits the site of Kiowa's death and leaves his moccasins as a memorial
to his friend.

Curt Lemon Lemon represents an outdated model of masculine
heroism. He is brave and fearless to a fault, known in Alpha Company for pulling crazy stunts just for the attention and the thrill of
danger. He even makes a dentist pull a healthy tooth from his
mouth to prove to everyone that he is not afraid of dentists. Eventually stepping on a booby trap kills him.

Lt. Jimmy Cross The leader of Alpha Company, Cross personifies mental escapism, the ability to project one's mind somewhere
else to escape from an undesirable situation. Instead of concen-
trating on the war, Cross occupies his mind with memories of
Martha, his old sweetheart. Rather than helping to search for
Kiowa's body, Cross spends time thinking about the letter he must
write to Kiowa's father. Cross meets up with O'Brien after the war,
and he still carries feelings of unrequited love for Martha. Whether
in the middle of the war or 20 years later, Cross focuses on life outside of war, but also carries a heavy, self-imposed burden of guilt
because of it.

Norman Bowker A foot soldier in Alpha Company, Bowker
embodies the effect known as "survivor guilt." He cannot forgive
himself for outliving his friends who died in battle. He feels intense
culpability for Kiowa's death and cannot adjust to civilian life in

his small hometown after the war. He wants O'Brien to write a story about a guy like him who cannot talk about his war-related trauma. Bowker eventually commits suicide.

Rat Kiley   The medic of Alpha Company, Rat represents the allure and the danger of storytelling. He is known for spinning yarns and making grotesque exaggerations. Rat helps O'Brien when he is shot for the first time. Rat's imagination eventually claims his sanity, as he begins to hallucinate in-country. He shoots himself, not to kill, but to be excused from war because of injury.

Azar   A foot soldier in Alpha Company, Azar is the wild man who enjoys war. He makes jokes about death, even the death of Kiowa. He mocks the movements of a traumatized Vietnamese girl dancing for fun and helps O'Brien play a cruel prank on Jorgenson. Azar's real allegiance is to war itself, not to his friends or his cause.

Henry Dobbins   Dobbins is a foot soldier in Alpha Company who symbolizes "America itself, big and strong...slow of foot but always plodding along." He is a large man with a soft heart who feels sympathy for others and anger against unwarranted cruelty. He has a keen sense of morality and treats everyone, enemies and friends, with respect.

Mitchell Sanders   The radio officer of Alpha Company, Sanders is the voice of soldierly experience and practical wisdom. He tells stories about how other soldiers react to Vietnam, and he vehemently blames Lt. Cross for Kiowa's death due to his incompetence as a leader.

Ted Lavender   A soldier in Alpha Company who represents emotional escapism from the war. He achieves this escapism through drug abuse and ultimately is killed.

Dave Jenson and Lee Strunk   These Alpha Company soldiers demonstrate the close relationship between aggression and camaraderie. They serve as foil for one another, each bringing the other to the edge of loyalty and violence. They make an agreement to kill the other should he sustain a permanently debilitating wound.

Bobby Jorgenson   The medic who replaces Rat Kiley, Jorgenson symbolizes the young, inexperienced, "green" soldier, or "FNG." When O'Brien is shot a second time, Jorgenson is too afraid to help him quickly, and O'Brien subsequently develops a hideous infection. O'Brien later gets revenge when he and Azar play mind tricks on Jorgenson.

Young soldier in the field   Representing naiveté and shock, this member of Alpha Company is talking to Kiowa when the attack begins that takes Kiowa's life. The next morning he cannot think of anything but the picture of his girlfriend lost in the attack.

Mary Anne Bell   Girlfriend to soldier Mark Fossie, she represents the corruption of innocence that takes place in war. She arrives wearing "white culottes and this sexy pink sweater," fresh from suburban U.S., and becomes a bestial instrument of death, scarier than even the Green Berets.

Mark Fossie   Medic at Tra Bong who brings his girlfriend, Mary Anne Bell, over to Vietnam from the U.S.

Eddie Diamond   Narcotic-addicted, highest-ranking officer in the Tra Bong area medic camp that Rat Kiley is temporarily assigned to with Mark Fossie and Mary Anne Bell.

North Vietnamese soldier   Soldier killed by "O'Brien." "O'Brien" invents an entire personal history for this soldier and feels shock and guilt for killing him. The soldier also appears in "O'Brien's" dreams years later.

Vietnamese girl   Traumatized sole survivor of a village, Alpha Company comes across this girl dancing in the midst of rubble and corpses.

Kathleen   Young daughter of "O'Brien" who accompanies him back to Vietnam and to the spot where Kiowa died. She cannot understand why her father cannot put the war behind him.

Linda   Fourth-grade girlfriend of "O'Brien." They saw a war movie on a date. She died from a brain tumor. Hers was the first dead body "O'Brien" saw.

Timmy   Fourth-grade persona of "Tim O'Brien" who felt a "deep and rich . . .love" for Linda.

Nick Veenhof   Fourth-grade classmate of "O'Brien" and Linda who, being a prankster, pulls Linda's hat off, revealing her bald head and surgery scars.

Lemon's sister   Curt Lemon's sister, who did not respond to Kiley's letter about her brother's death because, presumably, she found the letter's content disturbing and inappropriate.

Martha   Lt. Cross's love interest; he keeps her picture with him in Vietnam. She does not return his feelings. "O'Brien" suggests that she has a secret, possibly that she had been raped. She becomes a Lutheran missionary and does not want to be married.

Character Map

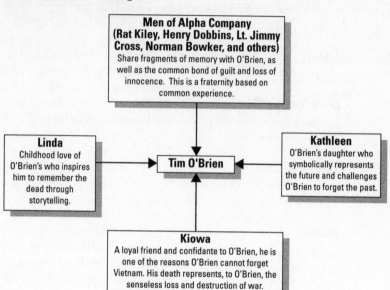

Men of Alpha Company (Rat Kiley, Henry Dobbins, Lt. Jimmy Cross, Norman Bowker, and others)
Share fragments of memory with O'Brien, as well as the common bond of guilt and loss of innocence. This is a fraternity based on common experience.

Linda
Childhood love of O'Brien's who inspires him to remember the dead through storytelling.

Tim O'Brien

Kathleen
O'Brien's daughter who symbolically represents the future and challenges O'Brien to forget the past.

Kiowa
A loyal friend and confidante to O'Brien, he is one of the reasons O'Brien cannot forget Vietnam. His death represents, to O'Brien, the senseless loss and destruction of war.

CRITICAL COMMENTARIES

The sections that follow provide great tools for supplementing your reading of *The Things They Carried*. First, in order to enhance your understanding of and enjoyment from reading, we provide quick summaries in case you have difficulty when you read the original literary work. Each summary is followed by commentary: literary devices, character analyses, themes, and so on. Keep in mind that the interpretations here are solely those of the author of this study guide and are used to jumpstart your thinking about the work. No single interpretation of a complex work like *The Things They Carried* is infallible or exhaustive, and you'll likely find that you interpret portions of the work differently from the author of this study guide. Read the original work and determine your own interpretations, referring to these Notes for supplemental meanings only.

The Things They Carried 22

Love 27

Spin 29

On the Rainy River 32

Enemies/Friends 38

How to Tell a True War Story 42

The Dentist 46

Sweetheart of Song Tra Bong 49

Stockings 53

Church 55

The Man I Killed/Ambush 57

Style 61

Speaking of Courage 63

Notes 67

In the Field 70

Good Form 73

Field Trip 75

The Ghost Soldiers 77

Night Life 82

The Lives of the Dead 84

The Things They Carried

Summary

An unnamed narrator describes in third person the thoughts and actions of Johnny Cross, the lieutenant of an Army unit on active combat duty in the Vietnam War. Lt. Cross is preoccupied by thoughts of Martha, a young woman he dated before he joined the Army. He thinks about letters she wrote him; he thinks about whether or not she is a virgin; he thinks about how much he loves her and wants her to love him. Her letters do not indicate that she feels the same way.

The narrator lists things that the soldiers carry with them, both tangible and intangible, such as Lt. Cross's picture of and feelings for Martha. Other members of the unit are introduced through descriptions of the things they carry, such as Henry Dobbins who carries extra food, Ted Lavender who carries tranquilizer pills, and Kiowa who carries a hunting hatchet. O'Brien introduces readers to the novel's primary characters by describing the articles that the soldiers carry. The level of detail O'Brien offers about the characters is expanded upon and illuminated in the chapters that follow, though O'Brien distills the essence of each characters' personality through the symbolic items each carries. Henry Dobbins carries a machine gun and his girlfriend's pantyhose. Dave Jensen carries soap, dental floss, foot powder, and vitamins. Mitchell Sanders carries condoms, brass knuckles, and the unit's radio. Norman Bowker carries a diary. Kiowa carries a volume of the New Testament and moccasins. Rat Kiley carries his medical kit, brandy, comic books, and M&M's candy. The narrator offers additional detail about selected items; for example, the poncho Ted Lavender carries will later be used by his fellow soldiers to carry his dead body.

This device is an example of the author and narrator embedding small details in the text that will be further explained later in the book. It is important to note, too, how the details are selective; they are recalled by a character, the unnamed narrator of the chapter. The details of what each man carries are funneled through the memory of this narrator.

O'Brien details at great length what all the men carry: standard gear, weapons, tear gas, explosives, ammunitions, entrenching tools, starlight scopes, grenades, flak jackets, boots, rations, and the Army newsletter.

They also carry their grief, terror, love, and longing, with poise and dignity. O'Brien's extended catalog of items creates a picture in the reader's mind that grows incrementally. O'Brien's technique also allows each character to be introduced with a history and a unique place within the group of men.

Lt. Cross is singled out from the group, and O'Brien offers the most detail about his interior feelings and thoughts. Many of these soldiers "hump," or carry, photographs, and Lieutenant Cross has an action shot of Martha playing volleyball. He also carries memories of their date and regrets that he did not try to satisfy his desire to become intimate with her by tying her up and touching her knee. O'Brien stresses that Lt. Cross carries all these things, but in addition carries the lives of his men.

Commentary

Even as O'Brien opens *The Things They Carried,* he sets forth the novel's primary themes of memory and imagination and the opportunity for mental escape that these powers offer. For example, as Lt. Cross moves through the rigorous daily motions of combat duty, his mind dwells on Martha. Importantly, as he thinks about Martha, he does not merely recall memories of her; instead he imagines what might be, such as "romantic camping trips" into the White Mountains in New Hampshire. O'Brien describes these longings of Lt. Cross as "pretending." Pretending is a form of storytelling, that is, telling stories to oneself. O'Brien underscores the importance of Lt. Cross's actions by emphasizing the artifacts—Martha's letters and photograph—and characterizes Lt. Cross as the carrier of these possessions as well as of his love for Martha.

O'Brien moves from employing the literary technique of describing the soldiers' physical artifacts to introducing the novel's primary characters. The minute details he provides about objects that individuals carry is telling, and particular attention should be paid to these details because they foreshadow the core narratives that comprise the novel. This technique of cataloging the things the soldiers carry also functions to create fuller composites of the characters, and by extension make the characters seem more real to readers.

This aesthetic of helping readers connect with his characters is O'Brien's primary objective in the novel, to make readers feel the story he presents as much as is physically and emotionally possible, as if it were real. Though the minutiae that O'Brien includes—for example the weight of a weapon, the weight of a radio, the weight of a grenade in ounces—seems superfluous, it is supposed to be accretive in his readers' imaginations so that they can begin to feel the physical weight of the burdens of war, as well as, eventually, the psychological and emotional burdens (so much as it is possible for a non-witness to war to perceive). O'Brien's attention to sensory detail also supports this primary objective of evoking a real response in the reader.

With Lavender's death, O'Brien creates a tension between the "actuality" of Lt. Cross's participation in battle and his interior, imagined fantasies that give him refuge. In burning Martha's letters and accepting blame for Lavender's death, Cross's conflicting trains of thought signal the reader to be cautious when deciding what is truth or fantasy and when assigning meaning to these stories. While he destroyed the physical accoutrements, the mementos of Martha, Lt. Cross continues to carry the memory of her with him. To that memory is also added the burden of grief and guilt. Despite this emotional burden, O'Brien, as he continues in the following chapter, begins to highlight the central question of the novel: Why people carry the things they do?

Glossary

(Here and in the following chapters, difficult words and phrases, as well as allusions and historical references, are explained.)

rucksack   A kind of knapsack strapped over the shoulders.

foxhole   A hole dug in the ground as a temporary protection for one or two soldiers against enemy gunfire or tanks.

perimeter   A boundary strip where defenses are set up.

heat tabs   Fuel pellets used for heating C rations.

C rations   A canned ration used in the field in World War II.

R & R   Rest and recuperation, leave.

Than Khe   (also Khe Sanh) A major battle in the Tet Offensive, the siege lasted well over a month in the beginning of 1968. Khe Sanh was thought of as an important strategic location for both the Americans and the North Vietnamese. American forces were forced to withdraw from Khe Sanh.

SOP   Abbreviation for standard operating procedure.

RTO   Radio telephone operator who carried a lightweight infantry field radio.

grunt   A U.S. infantryman.

hump   To travel on foot, especially when carrying and transporting necessary supplies for field combat.

platoon   A military unit composed of two or more squads or sections, normally under the command of a lieutenant: it is a subdivision of a company, troop, and so on.

medic   A medical noncommissioned officer who gives first aid in combat; aidman; corpsman.

M-60   American-made machine gun.

PFC   Abbreviation for Private First Class.

Spec 4   Specialist Rank, having no command function; soldier who carries out orders.

M-16   The standard American rifle used in Vietnam after 1966.

flak jacket   A vestlike, bulletproof jacket worn by soldiers.

KIA   Abbreviation for killed in action, to be killed in the line of duty.

chopper   A helicopter.

dustoff   Medical evacuation by helicopter.

Claymore antipersonnel mine   An antipersonnel mine that scatters shrapnel in a particular, often fan-shaped, area when it explodes.

Starlight scope   A night-vision telescope that enables a user to see in the dark.

tunnel complexes   The use of tunnels by the Viet Cong as hiding places, caches for food and weapons, headquarter complexes and protection against air strikes and artillery fire was a characteristic of the Vietnam war.

The Stars and Stripes   A newsletter-style publication produced for servicemen by the U.S. Army.

Bronze Star A U.S. military decoration awarded for heroic or meritorious achievement or service in combat not involving aerial flight.

Purple Heart A U.S. military decoration awarded to members of the armed forces wounded or killed in action by or against an enemy: established in 1782 and re-established in 1932.

entrenching tool A shovel-like tool, among its other uses, used to dig temporary fortifications such as foxholes.

zapped Killed.

freedom bird Any aircraft which returned servicemen to the U.S.

sin loi From Vietnamese, literally meaning excuse me, though servicemen came to understand the term as meaning too bad or tough luck.

Love

Summary

Character "Tim O'Brien," a middle-aged writer, recalls when, many years after the war, Lt. Jimmy Cross visits him at his home. They spend a full day looking at old photographs and talking, recalling both good and bad memories of the war. "O'Brien" asks Jimmy about Martha. He is surprised when Jimmy produces the photograph of Martha playing volleyball in a small frame, because he thought Jimmy had burned it after one of his men died. Jimmy had, but he saw Martha years later at a high school reunion and she eventually gave him a replacement photograph. He had told her that he still loved her and was curious about why she never married but became a Lutheran missionary. She said she did not know, but she intimated that there was a reason why. All night long Jimmy told her about how he wanted to touch her knee. Martha told him that she could not understand why men did such things. After learning this, "O'Brien" steers the conversation away from Martha. As Jimmy is leaving, "O'Brien" says that he would like to write a story about their visit. Jimmy begins to ask "O'Brien" not to mention something in his story, but "O'Brien" interrupts him and says that he will not.

Commentary

This chapter is rich with subtext about Martha that is continued from the preceding chapter. In "The Things They Carried," Lt. Cross is preoccupied with thoughts of Martha: When checking on Lee Strunk who is searching a tunnel, "suddenly, without willing it, he was thinking about Martha. . . . he tried to concentrate on Lee Strunk and the war, all the dangers, but his love was too much for him." "The Things They Carried" is a story about longing, Lt. Cross's longing for Martha's love; "Love" is a story about longing as well. In this chapter, however, Lt. Cross longs for what could never have been, compared to his hopeful longings while he was in-country, which helped him both to maintain his ability to face the discomforts and horrors of war and to question his competence because of his constant thoughts of Martha.

In offering more details about Martha—that she became a Lutheran missionary, that she had never married, that she did not know why she had not—including her remark about how men do "those things," the author subtly reveals that Martha had been the victim of rape. This detail connects to Lt. Cross's fixation on her virginity in the preceding chapter; it undoes the "reality" of Lt. Cross's fantasies by making his wish that she was a virgin an impossible "reality," and therefore begins to undo the reader's sense of what is truth or fantasy. O'Brien demonstrates the complicated relationship between truth and fantasy in the final sentence of the chapter when "O'Brien," the narrator, promises not to mention the burden Martha carries, the rape that is alluded to, but still makes it the crux of the chapter. Thus the focus of the entire vignette remains unmentioned.

Literary Device

Another central theme of the novel emerges in this chapter as well: the "O'Brien" persona. A persona is a person created by the author to tell a story; the persona does not necessarily share the attitudes or dispositions of the actual author. Noting this fictional divide between the "O'Brien" persona and the actual author, Tim O'Brien, is crucial to understanding the novel. The preceding chapter is presented in *third-person omniscient,* in which the narrator tells the story using third person and is free to disclose the thoughts and emotions of characters. This chapter shifts to *first person,* in which the story is told by a character of the story and from that character's limited point of view. The persona, middle-aged writer Tim O'Brien, now becomes a subjective filter through which readers gain information. O'Brien reminds readers of this filter as "O'Brien" promises not to disclose Martha's rape.

Glossary

Bonnie and Clyde   A 1967 film starring Warren Beatty and Faye Dunaway about the criminal pair of lovers.

Spin

Summary

"O'Brien" offers in his memoirs a group of related fragments of stories, or memory snapshots. He recalls Mitchell Sanders mailing his body lice to his local draft board. He remembers Norman Bowker and Henry Dobbins's nightly checkers games. "O'Brien" narrates what it is like to sit at his typewriter and remember these episodes from his experiences in Vietnam, and what it is like to read what he has written about them. He recalls the bad memories, and he recalls the good memories, such as those of the old Vietnamese man who led his unit through a dangerous minefield.

"O'Brien" continues to think about his memories from the vantage of being a writer. His daughter wonders why he writes about Vietnam, but these stories and fragments stick in his memory and bring his past into the present of his life. Finally he suggests that stories will remain, even when memory of what actually happened is erased.

Commentary

Literary
Device

O'Brien offers his readers a series of fragmented scenes, like verbal snapshots, as a way to comment on the act of memory (in general) and on the act of remembering the Vietnam War (specifically). He presents the war as an event marked by the disorder of anti-war demonstration and military mismanagement. This mode of fragmented expression, the medium O'Brien chooses to use in this chapter and in the novel over all, is the message. That is, the nature of memory is fragmentary; people do not tend to remember an event in a narrative beginning-to-end fashion. Rather, O'Brien suggests that "what sticks to memory, often, are those odd little fragments that have no beginning and no end."

O'Brien demonstrates this fragmentation by hopping between a wide variety of stories—the Vietnamese guide, Mitchell Sanders mailing his lice, Ted Lavender adopting a puppy—within the space of few pages. Also note this fragmenting effect on the chapter level of the novel;

the novel is not marked by a continuity in which one chapter flows logically into the next, as is the form in traditional narrative novels or autobiographies. O'Brien does not set the path of memory and remembering as one that can be traversed easily (which O'Brien demonstrates through the metaphor of the minefield and his mention of the nightly checkers game). War, and by extension, memory of war and storytelling about war, is not orderly, and its meaning is not able to be captured through a pedestrian beginning-to-end narration.

Style & Language

The fragmented style of the chapters also operates on a second meta-fictive level, carrying the medium-is-the-message metaphor further. As "O'Brien" describes the Vietnam War combat experience, he emphasizes that the routine and daily life of a soldier was marked by similar abrupt shifts in action: "Well, you'd think, this isn't so bad. And right then you'd hear gunfire behind you. . . ." O'Brien adopts this fragmentary style, thus forcing his readers to feel a version of this trepidation caused by the uncertainty of what is coming next. O'Brien's primary objective for storytelling is to evoke a visceral response in his reader.

Theme

Another major point to note in this chapter is the way the jumping between thoughts and memories connects the narrator's past and present. An example of this is "O'Brien's" mention of his daughter Kathleen's suggestion that he forget about the war. Forgetting is not a possibility for O'Brien, which should be clear to the reader, as O'Brien demonstrates his inability to forget by telling us the story in the first place. Forgetting stands in direct opposition to the fragmentary model of remembering that O'Brien describes. The fragments, like the sudden sound of gunfire, suddenly appear, but without O'Brien invoking them or conjuring them up in his mind.

"O'Brien" suggests that people remember the past (and, how, incidentally, he gets ideas to write): "You take your material where you find it, which is in your life, at the intersection of past and present." Presumably, a little girl's memory—Kathleen's—is not too broad, and her present is filled with thoughts of getting a pony, but for O'Brien, the force of his war memories make the past his present, like a series of post-traumatic-disorder flashbacks or constant survivor guilt. As an author, as he commits his memories into words, he symbolically transports his past into the present. This continual uninvited "re-memory" intrudes on the ability of veterans such as O'Brien, Lt. Cross, and Norman Bowker to forget the past.

Finally, as O'Brien suggests in the closing paragraph, stories are a way to impose order on the fragments that crop up, "for joining the past to the future." O'Brien continues to explore this major theme of remembering using the act of storytelling to arrange and understand fragments in later chapters.

Glossary

FREE   Designation written by servicemen in the upper-right corner of an envelope in place of stamps; soldiers were allowed to mail items free of charge.

Poppa-san   An old Vietnamese man.

in the pink   In good physical condition; healthy; fit.

AWOL   Absent without leave.

Da Nang   Seaport in central Vietnam, on the South China Sea; many battalions were stationed there.

truth goose   A fictitious story that feels as real as the truth.

bodybag   A rubberized bag sealed with a zipper, used for transporting a dead body from a war zone, accident, etc.

paddies   Rice fields.

buck sergeant stripes   Embroidered patches sewn on to uniforms to signify the enlisted army rank, also known as E5.

My Khe   A huge beach nestled between a forest and the Kinh River.

On the Rainy River

Summary

In an attempt to relieve some shame and guilt about his involvement in the war, middle-aged writer "O'Brien" relates a story about himself that he has never before told anyone. "O'Brien's" story is about the summer of 1968 when he was 21 years old and was drafted to serve in the Army. Before his draft notice arrived, "O'Brien" had taken a mild stand against the war in the form of campaigning for the presidential campaign of anti-war advocate Eugene McCarthy and writing college newspaper editorials against the war.

He recounts his thoughts on receiving a draft notice, feeling that he was not suited for war because his educational accomplishments and graduate school prospects were too great. O'Brien tells his father that his plan for the summer is to wait and work. He spends his summer working at a pig slaughterhouse and meatpacking plant. The work is messy and unpleasant, and O'Brien feels his life going out of control.

Around mid-July, O'Brien begins thinking about crossing the border into Canada to avoid the draft. He weighs the morality of this decision as he fears losing respectability, being ridiculed, and being caught by authorities.

While at work in the slaughterhouse, O'Brien suddenly feels an urge to go to Canada. He leaves work and drives north along the Rainy River, the natural border between the U.S. and Canada. Exhausted and scared, O'Brien stops, still on the U.S. side of the border, at a shabby old fishing resort. The elderly owner, Elroy Berdahl, rents him a cabin. Elroy does not pry into O'Brien's plans, though they are probably fairly obvious. O'Brien continues to feel nervousness and fear, and above all else, shame for running to Canada, but he joins Elroy in chores around the lodge to forget about his troubles.

When figuring O'Brien's bill, Elroy recalls the chores O'Brien had done, decides that instead he owes O'Brien money, and gives him $200. O'Brien refuses the money, though he would need it if he did continue on to Canada. But Elroy tacks it to O'Brien's cabin door with a note marked "Emergency Fund."

During O'Brien's last day at the lodge, Elroy takes him fishing on the river. O'Brien the narrator comments on the thoughts that flashed through his mind. He remembers crying and feeling helpless while Elroy just keeps on fishing, pretending not to notice. O'Brien tries to force himself out of the boat and toward the Canadian shore but can not compel himself to flee to Canada. They return to the lodge, and O'Brien departs for home and, eventually, for Vietnam.

Commentary

From the first sentence of the chapter, O'Brien begins to impress, however subtly, the importance of the novel's form, a blend of war autobiography and writer's memoir. Readers should note that a writer's memoir is a form of autobiography. Generally, a writer's memoir is more essayistic and contemplative than an autobiography, in which an author recounts scenes from his or her own life. Writer's memoirs frequently describe how a writer writes and what the conditions were—mental and emotional—that surrounded the production of some literary or journalistic work. The admission that "this is one story I've never told before" signals two points to the reader. First, the story establishes a confessional tone and creates an immediate empathy between the reader and the O'Brien character. Second, in the context of the preceding chapter, the reader knows that this is an unresolved story, perhaps a fragment of memory that, given O'Brien's philosophy of storytelling, is being crafted into a story as a means for understanding the events of the past.

Style &
Language

Yet the story is not fragmentary and disconnected, abruptly moving between memories. The overall form of the chapter is narrative, though the stream-of-consciousness interjection of raw emotions interrupts the story's fluidity. For example, when O'Brien discusses the justifications that apparently underpinned U.S. involvement in the war, he writes that "the very facts were shrouded in uncertainty" and that "the only certainty that summer was moral confusion." This political discourse O'Brien provides is the real-world macrocosm version of the personal microcosm of "moral uncertainty" that distressed him during the summer of 1968. The uncertainty continues to disturb him until he takes this "act of remembrance" and makes sense of moral disorder by committing it to paper and formulating it into a story for the narrator himself and the novel's readers to understand.

An important difference exists between the physical and sensory detail O'Brien employs at the beginning of the chapter, or rather the lack of it, and the attention paid to it at the chapter's close. "O'Brien" describes his stance against the war as "almost entirely an intellectual activity. . . . I felt no personal danger." His precise use of detail mirrors an internal change in O'Brien as he is described in physical detail.

An example of this detail is the contrast of O'Brien's work in the meatpacking plant to the future that he hopes awaits him in graduate school. O'Brien works in the meatpacking plant as a summer job, not as an occupation that will become a full-time career. He has aspirations, and those aspirations are higher than working in such conditions. Work in the plant, for O'Brien, is nearly an indignity, an indignity that is surpassed only by his participation in a war that he morally opposes. O'Brien offers this variation in detail for the following reason: the former, with its "dense greasy pig-stink," elicits a strong reaction from the reader. The effect also appears when Elroy Berdahl perceptively tells O'Brien that he had wondered about the smell. The metaphor of the pork product assembly line also extends to the military machine that drafts soldiers and sends them to war.

O'Brien only took action to evade the draft and follow his own inclinations rather than follow the expectations of his community after he "felt something break open in [his] chest...a physical rupture—a cracking-leaking-popping feeling." O'Brien reprises this idea when "O'Brien" revisits the shit field ("Field Trip") and when Timmy/O'Brien learns of Linda's death ("The Lives of the Dead"). He creates a complex relationship between physical detail, his ability to understand the story of his own life, and the audience's ability to understand the vicarious lessons of war, even if those lessons are paradoxical.

Theme

O'Brien sets up paradoxical relationships that are revisited in various forms throughout the novel. One such paradox is that of courage and fear. He explains that he was "ashamed to be doing the right thing" in following his conscience and going to Canada. Because this paradox is a reversal of commonly held notions about courage in war, O'Brien—who has never told the story of his flight to the Tip Top Lodge before—needs to "write" a story as a means for structuring a way to understand the paradox and come to terms with it.

This meta-fictive means of imposing meaning on moral disorder and personal conflict is not the only storytelling O'Brien does in this chapter. He actually tries to do the same thing in the middle of the

Rainy River—he "slipped out of his own skin" and watched himself (much like Elroy Berdahl watched and read O'Brien) in his attempts to decide whether he should escape to Canada. At the end of the chapter, however, the importance of the physicality of "O'Brien" reemerges. O'Brien was literally paralyzed as he tried to force himself from the boat. So it follows that he had denied his own feelings and submitted to the schemas of stories of other people, like the older generation of veterans whom he despises, and to what he considered cowardice—at least until finally telling this story.

Glossary

The Lone Ranger   Famous cowboy hero and the star of first a radio show and then a television show in the 1940s and 1950s.

USS *Maddox*   American destroyer stationed in the Gulf of Tonkin.

Gulf of Tonkin   Arm of the South China Sea between Hainan Island and the coasts of Southern China and Northern Vietnam. Location where North Vietnamese forces attacked and sunk two American ships in 1964. Afterwards, Congress passed the Gulf of Tonkin Resolution, authorizing military action in Southeast Asia.

Ho Chi Minh   (1890–1969; born Nguyen That Thanh) President of North Vietnam (1954–1969).

Geneva Accords   Established in 1954, the Geneva Accords were rules which governed military action and treatment of captured soldiers.

SEATO   Southeast Asia Treaty Organization (1955–1976).

Cold War   Hostility and sharp conflict as in diplomacy and economics between states, without actual warfare.

dominoes   Refers here to the "domino effect" or "domino theory," which was the prevalent course of foreign policy adopted by the United States during the Cold War. The notion was that if one area or nation "fell" to Communist forces, that the surrounding areas would also "fall" under Communist influences, like dominoes toppling over.

Gene McCarthy (b. 1916) Eugene McCarthy, a World War II veteran, served in the U.S. House of Representatives from 1948 to 1958 and the U.S. Senate from 1958 to 1968. In 1968, he ran for the Democratic presidential nomination, winning the New Hampshire primary, a factor in Lyndon Johnson's decision not to seek reelection. McCarthy supported the Vietnam War at first, voting in favor of the Gulf of Tonkin Resolution, but by 1968, he strongly opposed the war.

draft notice Official notice sent by the Selective Service System, informing a young man to report for an armed forces physical exam. The first step to being drafed into the armed forces.

Phi Beta Kappa An honorary society of U.S. college students in liberal arts and sciences with high scholastic rank; a member of this society.

summa cum laude With the greatest praise: a phrase signifying above-average academic standing at the time of graduation from a college or university: the highest of three categories.

jingo A person who boasts of his patriotism and favors an aggressive, threatening, warlike foreign policy; chauvinist.

graduate school deferment Men in graduate school who maintained a high enough GPA (grade point average) could defer the draft and remain in school in the U.S.

National Guard In the U.S., the organized militia forces of the individual states, a component of the Army of the U.S. when called into active federal service.

reserves Personnel or units in the armed forces not on active duty but subject to call; last resort troops, usually remained in the U.S.

CO Conscientious objector. A designation for legal exemption from military combat service due to moral or personal ideological conflict.

Bao Dai (1913–1997, meaning "Keeper or Preserver of Greatness") Bao Dai was the last of the Nguyen Emperors.

Diem Ngo Dinh Diem (1901–1963), first president of South Vietnam (1955–1963).

Saint George Patron saint of England.

LBJ   Lyndon B. Johnson (1908–1973) 36th president of the United States (1963–1969).

Huck Finn   Protagonist from the novel *The Adventures of Tom Sawyer* by Mark Twain marked by his plucky and rebellious spirit.

Abbie Hoffman   (1936–1989) A countercultural icon of the 1960s, Abbie Hoffman was successful at turning many flower children into political activists.

Jane Fonda   (b. 1937) Actress and sex symbol who toured Vietnam in 1972; she became a vocal anti-war activist and was harshly criticized by some veterans for her political position on the war.

Gary Cooper   (1901–1961) film actor characterized by a rugged masculine quality well known for his roles in Westerns such as *High Noon* (1952). He also appeared in *For Whom the Bell Tolls* (1943) and *Sergeant York* (1941).

Plato's Republic   Central text of Western thought in which the Greek philosopher Plato outlines the construction of the ideal political city and leader.

Enemies/
Friends

Summary

On patrol, Lee Strunk and Dave Jensen fight over Jensen's missing jackknife, which he presumed Strunk stole. Jensen easily overpowers Strunk, hitting him repeatedly and breaking his nose. Because of this, Jensen starts to worry, growing anxious of what revenge Strunk might take on him. He keeps track of Strunk, paying attention to his whereabouts and being cautious of him when Strunk handles weapons. This tension builds up in Jensen, and he is continually nervous, until he eventually snaps and begins firing his weapon into the air, yelling Strunk's name. Later that night, Jensen borrows a pistol and uses it to break his own nose. He shows Strunk what he has done and asks whether they were now even; Strunk says sure. The next morning, Strunk can't stop laughing; he had stolen the jackknife.

Over the next month, Jensen and Strunk begin to pair up on ambushes together and cover each other on patrol. They slowly build up their friendship and trust. They draw up a pact that says if either one of them is badly wounded, that the other would kill him. They both sign the agreement. A few months later, Strunk is severely injured when he steps on a rigged mortar round. The blast of the explosion severs his right leg at the knee. A medic treats Strunk and prepares him for evacuation. Jensen goes to Strunk before he is evacuated out, and as Strunk opens his eyes and sees Jensen, he pleads with him not to kill him. Jensen tries to say some encouraging words, and swears not to follow their agreement and kill Strunk. Strunk is evacuated by helicopter, but the unit learns later that he had died in transit. O'Brien thinks this news brought relief to Jensen, who felt a heavy burden.

Commentary

O'Brien presents the story of a fight within a war, making us focus initially on the difference between a war and a fight. The fight is in some ways a microcosm to the macrocosm of Vietnam; both are violent engagements, both pit enemies against one another, and both have rules that are often ignored by the participants. O'Brien shows some of the similarities between the two, such as the seeming randomness of the quarrel between Strunk and Jensen in the "Enemies" vignette, and Strunk stepping on a mortar bomb in the sister vignette, "Friends." O'Brien says that the fight was over "something stupid—a missing jackknife," but however meaningless the reason, the fight was nonetheless a vicious engagement between two foes.

In addition to the randomness of Vietnam, O'Brien highlights the meaninglessness of it by beginning the description of the fight with the jackknife and by using the vignette as a metaphor for this meaninglessness that the characters feel. Strunk laughs uncontrollably when Jensen breaks his own nose out of fear for what Strunk might do in retaliation, and admits that he in fact did steal the knife. He laughs because Jensen breaking his nose has no meaning—Jensen was justified in his attacking Strunk in the first place. The uselessness of his gesture, motivated by fear, causes us to view the entire fight as void of meaning. We can then apply this model to Vietnam, seeing how the larger battle, no matter who wins or loses, will be meaningless.

On the other hand, O'Brien shows how the microcosm/macrocosm model fails by making the fight and the war different. First, the fight is more personal and emotional, for example, than Strunk stepping on a mortar bomb. Strunk gets his nose broken because of a fight, because his enemy relentlessly beat him and crushed his bones; he loses his leg for no reason other than where he stepped. He could not have known or prevented it, and anyone in the company could have the same happen at any moment. The fight is personal, between two opponents; the war is not. What the war lacks is a visible opponent, a physical enemy. When Strunk and Jensen fight, the quarrel becomes emotional and out-of-control because they have both yearned for a real enemy to touch, see, and destroy. In other words, Strunk and Jensen find in their opponent the physical presence that that war has denied them.

Because of the realness of a physical opponent, everything is more intense. Jensen's inability to relax is an example of how the fight is more pressing, more real to him than the war. After all, should a soldier be more afraid of one of his own company, even someone with whom he has had an argument, than an entire country of men who would shoot him on sight? Probably not, but the proximity and physicality of his new "enemy" fills Jensen with greater fear than all the Viet Cong. Likewise, the pact that Jensen and Strunk form is an extension of this personal side of war. O'Brien tells us that they did not become friends per se, but they learned to trust one another enough to form a death pact. Yet even though this was a sign of trust between two men, they still insisted on drawing it up on paper, signing it, and getting witnesses. They trusted each other enough to end their lives but not enough to go without public ratification of their pact.

In the end, when Strunk loses his leg, his fear of Jensen killing him is absolute. He does not appeal to any in his company who knew of the pact, just Jensen, whom he insists swear not to kill him. Ironically, the oath is enough to appease Strunk, where earlier an oath would not suffice; the desperateness of his situation forces him to take Jensen's promise on faith alone. Trust, then, depends on the situation, not on the person. Strunk trusts Jensen not to kill him on his word, but he would not trust him to make the original pact without a compact. O'Brien makes us wonder whom you can trust in a war.

The "Friends" vignette wraps up with Jensen violating his original pledge and not killing Strunk. Yet when news of Strunk's death comes to him, it "seemed to relieve Dave Jensen of an enormous weight." Jensen had gone back on his word and failed his friend, thus making himself no good friend to Strunk. Perhaps because he had not been severely wounded, Jensen had not undergone the same transformation that Strunk had, wishing for a life after a massive and debilitating wound more than the death of a soldier. Either way, Strunk's death fulfills Jensen's promise not to let either of them live after sustaining such a wound. He is able again to be Strunk's friend not through his actions, but through fate and his inaction. O'Brien forces us to question what is right and wrong in a war. If Jensen had lived up to his pledge, he would be a murderer. By failing to do it, even at Strunk's behest, he proves himself no friend. O'Brien makes us wonder which is worse.

Glossary

jackknife   A large pocketknife.

LZ Gator   Landing zone south of Chu Lai.

pull guard   To be assigned to a sentinel shift, to keep watch.

wheelchair wound   A permanently debilitating wound, especially loss of limbs or wounds which would cause paralysis.

rigged mortar round   A short-range weapon that fires a shell on a high trajectory.

How to Tell a True War Story

Summary

O'Brien offers a story about Rat Kiley that he assures his readers is true: Rat's friend, Curt Lemon, is killed, and Rat writes Lemon's sister a letter. Rat's letter talks about her brother and the crazy stunts he attempted. Rat believes the letter is poignant and personal; however, from Lemon's sister's viewpoint, it is inappropriate and disturbing. The sister never writes back, and Rat is offended and angered, as the reader is left to infer as the sister never returns the letter.

O'Brien suggests that Lemon's sister's failure to return the letter offers a kind of sad and true moral to the story. Lemon's death, an accident resulting from a game of catch with a grenade, is described in detail. O'Brien remembers body parts strewn in the jungle trees and thinks about his own memories of the event. He comments that in true stories it is difficult to distinguish what actually happened from what seemed to happen, again blurring the line between truth and story.

O'Brien offers readers the advice that they should be skeptical, and offers a story told to him by Mitchell Sanders as an example. A patrol goes into the mountains for a weeklong operation to monitor enemy movement. The jungle is spooky, and the men start hearing strange, eerie noises which become an opera, a glee club, chanting, and so on, but the voices they hear are not human. Sanders says that the mountains, trees, and rocks were making the noise, and that the men called in massive firepower. He says a colonel later asked them why, and they do not answer because they know he will not understand their story. Sanders says that the moral is that nobody listens; the next day Sanders admits he made up parts of the story.

Next, O'Brien tells what following Lemon's death: the unit comes across a baby water buffalo. Rat Kiley tries to feed it but it does not eat, so Kiley steps back and shoots the animal in its knee. Though crying, he continues to shoot the buffalo, aiming to hurt rather than kill it. Others dump the near dead buffalo in a well to kill it. O'Brien concludes that a true war story, like the one about the water buffalo, is never about war; these stories are about love, memory, and sorrow.

Commentary

O'Brien offers abstract commentary on storytelling and blurs the divisions between truth and fiction and author and authorial persona through a series of paradoxical reversals. The primary examples are the paragraphs that begin and end the chapter. O'Brien immediately brands the story as true. In a direct address to readers he claims, "this is true." In the final paragraphs, O'Brien reverses this claim by redefining truth. "None of it happened," he writes, "none of it." Central to understanding the chapter is charting O'Brien's progression of calling the story absolutely true to calling the veracity of the story and the reliability of the "O'Brien" persona narrator into question. O'Brien does not lie—he changes the definition of telling the truth.

In this vignette, O'Brien presents two stories that fail to be "true" to their intended audiences. The first example is the "few stories" Rat Kiley includes in his letter to Curt Lemon's sister. To Rat, these stories about Lemon's extreme and questionable acts are true, and he wants to convey this truth to the sister, who fails to respond because she understands the stories in completely antithetical ways.

Rat Kiley and Lemon's sister belong to different interpretive communities; they have different sets of experiences and expectations that they use to understand stories. The result is a radical difference in how they understand and feel the same "actual" events of a story. O'Brien carries this idea of competing communities of interpretation over to the text, which he demonstrates through his appraisal of the response of the woman who tells him she likes the story of the buffalo. She doesn't get the real truth of the story, which is Rat's fraternal love for Lemon, because she belongs to a different interpretive community.

O'Brien is commenting on readers and hearers of stories. Readers must remember that they are reading a story, by a fictional author, about listening to stories and can, unlike Lemon's sister, feel a personal response to the story's outcome. The story takes on a message of truth because of the context of the unanswered letter. On the one hand, Lemon's sister does respond, but on the other hand, her response is in the act of not answering Rat's letter. It is this action that makes the reader align his or her sympathies with Rat, and that solicitation of feeling from the reader is what makes the story "true." The story, O'Brien writes, "[is] so incredibly sad and true: she never wrote back."

The second story that fails to connect its meaning with its hearer is the fantastic and spooky story that Mitchell Sanders tells about the squad who was assigned to listen for signs of enemy movement. Just as O'Brien does in the chapter's first sentence, Sanders emphasizes that the story is true because it actually happened. Even though Sanders admits that he embellished the story—and that it technically is not "true" because it did not actually happen—this is irrelevant to O'Brien. Given the criteria on which he bases the "truth" of stories, Sanders's story has a kernel of truth in it: It is nearly true. O'Brien writes, "I could tell how desperately Sanders wanted me to believe him, his frustration at not quite getting the details right, not quite pinning down the final and definitive truth."

Literary Device

In this sense, O'Brien's analysis of Sanders's story recalls the title of the chapter, "How to Tell a True War Story." It suggests a second meaning to be applied to the readers and hearers of stories: that readers and hearers can "tell," or discern, stories that hold a truth, regardless of whether the events of the story actually occurred, based on certain criteria. According to O'Brien, the truth of a story depends solely on the audience hearing it told.

Style & Language

The common denominator for O'Brien is finally "gut instinct. A true war story, if truly told, makes the stomach believe." O'Brien demonstrates this idea by employing repetition. A noteworthy example is the four varying accounts of Curt Lemon's death within the chapter. Each retelling is embellished until finally a "true" version emerges that viscerally affects "O'Brien," and by extension, the reader. The details of O'Brien's nightmare flashback—Dave Jensen singing "Lemon Tree"—cinch the story as true. O'Brien assents that "truth" is gauged by the responses stories evoke: ". . . if I could ever get the story right. . . then you would believe the last thing Curt Lemon believed, which for him must've been the final truth." O'Brien revives the trope of metanarrative commentary as the story has been recreated in this fictional writer's memoir, which is in fact not true, but true enough to move the reader to identify emotionally with O'Brien and to share in his experiences through the use of imagination and sympathy.

Glossary

cooze   A derogatory name for a woman.

yellow mother   To be a coward or have failure of nerve.

Quang Ngai   City and province near Da Nang.

listening post (LP)   An advanced, concealed position near the enemy's lines, for detecting the enemy's movements by listening. Here, a three-man post placed outside the barbed wire surrounding a firebase to detect enemy movement in order to warn and defend the perimeter.

Radio Hanoi   Like National Public Radio in the U.S., Radio Hanoi was a national radio broadcast. Jane Fonda spoke on Radio Hanoi during her visit to Vietnam in 1972.

gook   Slang term for a person of East Asian descent, here meaning, specifically, a Vietnamese.

arty   Artillery.

air strikes   Air attacks on a ground or naval target.

napalm   Sodium palmitate or an aluminum soap added to gasoline or oil to form a jellylike substance; used in flame throwers and bombs.

Cobras   A type of helicopter used to attack enemy troops.

F-4s   Also called the Phantom II, a type of tactical fighter bomber widely used in the Vietnam War.

Willie Peter   White phosphorus mortar or artillery rounds.

HE   High explosive.

tracer rounds   A harmless projectile that lights a path for soldiers to aim projectile weaponry.

illumination rounds   Flares dropped from above or fired from the ground used to light up an area during darkness.

Lemon Tree   A song popularized in the 1960s by folk music group Peter, Paul and Mary. The song tells of a father warning his son about falling in love too deeply with a seemingly ideal girl, with the cautionary moral being that what appears sweet may actually be sour.

puffery   Exaggerated praise.

The Dentist

Summary

O'Brien remembers that when Curt Lemon died he found it difficult to mourn, as he did not know him well. He remembers Lemon's tendency to play the clichéd role of the macho soldier, deliberately taking unnecessary risks and bragging and embellishing them with untruths. O'Brien offers this story as a means for guarding against sentimentality over the dead: The unit of soldiers had been in an area that was relatively quiet, with no direct combat with the enemy and no casualties. An Army dentist visits the area to administer care to the unit. Though the dentist has only rudimentary facilities, Lemon is especially scared because of childhood experiences with dentists. He faints in the dentist's tent before being examined. Others in the unit know about this because they help get him on a cot after the episode. Lemon keeps to himself but can not let what happened go unanswered. He complains about a toothache and has the dentist pull a tooth without finding a problem with it, which pleases him and helps him recover from his embarrassment.

Commentary

Theme

A recurring theme in *The Things They Carried* is the investigation and problematization of ideas such as courage, heroism, and valor. In this vignette, O'Brien again takes up the notion of memory and makes us question how we honor the memory of war and war heroes. The opening line of the story immediately confronts us with paradox: "When Curt Lemon was killed, I found it hard to mourn." We expect someone to mourn a fallen comrade, especially a fellow soldier, but O'Brien will not because, he leads us to believe, Curt Lemon did not earn the right to be mourned. So then, we must ask what must someone do in order to be mourned? In response, O'Brien gives us the story of Lemon and the Army dentist, giving his audience the opportunity to judge whether Lemon deserves mourning or not.

The story of Lemon and the dentist is a simple one with complex implications. Lemon is a braggart and relishes creating a machismo personality. His weakness is that he needs others to hold him in awe, to treat him as important. It is upon this weakness, as O'Brien sees it, that the story pivots and O'Brien's low opinion of Lemon is based.

The setting is a relaxed environment that comes close to the description of a vacation. There is no impending fear, no looming threat of attack, and in this setting Lemon finds himself out of sorts. As O'Brien frequently does, he makes the appearance of the dentist a seemingly random event, denying us the ability to find constant meaning in the war and its mechanisms. Lemon is shown not to be high strung or brave, but childish, reverting to fears sustained as a child about dentists. These fears overpower him even as an adult, a man, a soldier. So potent are the fears of youth that they can weaken even the man who tries harder than anyone to appear strong. Lemon does not even fight against seeing the dentist, but instead faints and quietly is carried away.

Character Insight

He returns, however, to have the dentist treat a fictional toothache and pull a healthy tooth. Lemon cannot cope with letting his childhood fears master his adult life, so he confronts them artificially. In the end, though, his adventure does not erase his initial failure; while he may have ultimately faced his fears, he shrank from them in front of his company and then returned to confront them not out of a new-found sense of courage, but out of stubborn pride. He was still afraid of the dentist, but was now more afraid of losing the image he had worked so hard to create for himself. In other words, he exchanged one fear for another, still letting his fears control him.

For this reason, O'Brien does not feel that Lemon earned mourning rights. If we believe that we should mourn the dead, how does someone earn that right? O'Brien does not mourn Lemon, but could he not mourn Lemon the boy who never outgrew fear? But the large issue at hand for O'Brien is that we tend to mourn people because they died, paying no attention to how they lived; we tend to memorialize soldiers for being soldiers, war for being war. O'Brien's refusal to mourn a dead man, a soldier, a fellow of his company shocks us and makes us rethink how we treat the dead and how we might warp the truth of a man when we try to honor his memory.

Glossary

Chu Lai   Site where many troops were stationed.

AO   Area of operations.

dog tag   A military identification tag worn about the neck.

Sweetheart of Song Tra Bong

Summary

O'Brien recalls a story of Rat Kiley's. Though Rat swears the story is true, O'Brien doubts its accuracy. He explains that Rat exaggerates not because he wants to deceive, but because he wants listeners to almost feel the story so that it seems more real. Rat had been assigned to a medical detachment near Tra Bong in an area the medics shared with six Green Berets. The groups did not interact often. During an all-night drinking session, a medic jokingly mentions that the medics should pool their money and import some prostitutes from Saigon. One medic, Mark Fossie, is taken by the idea, and six weeks later his high school sweetheart, Mary Anne Bell, arrives at the compound.

Young and naïve, Mary Anne insists on learning about Vietnamese culture and the Vietnam War up close. She assists when the medical unit receives casualties. Eventually she stops wearing make-up, and her attention is consumed by learning how to use an M-16 assault rifle. Fossie suggests that she return home, but she does not. She begins staying out late, finally staying out all night. Fossie, realizing Mary Anne is missing, wakes up Rat. They search for her but do not find her.

O'Brien interrupts the story to comment on how Rat told the story. Rat would stop with Mary Anne's disappearance and ask where she might be. Mitchell Sanders guesses that she was with the Green Berets because Rat mentioned them, and that is how stories work. Rat would resume the story and tell his listeners that she was resting with the Green Berets in their hootch after an all-night ambush.

The next morning Mary Anne returns wearing green fatigues and carrying a rifle. She tells Fossie that they will talk later, but he is angry and will not wait. Later that day, Mary Anne appears fully groomed, wearing her feminine clothes. Fossie explains that they officially became engaged, and the pair maintains a façade of happiness. Fossie makes arrangements for Mary Anne's trip home. The next morning she disappears again with the Green Berets. Three weeks pass until she returns. The next day Fossie waits outside the Green Berets' area, waiting to see Mary Anne. He hears an eerie human voice. Pushing inside the Green

Berets' hootch, he sees piles of bones, smells a horrendous stench, and hears Mary Anne chanting. She tells Fossie that she likes this life and that he does not belong there.

Rat's platoon buddies dislike the abrupt ending and ask what happened to Mary Anne. He tells them that the rest is hearsay, but that he understands that she disappeared into the jungle.

Commentary

Theme

Like many of O'Brien's stories, this one is not really about what it seems to be about. This is not a story about Mary Anne and her transformation—it is a story about storytelling and the loss of innocence. The meta-textual discussion is about storytelling, the dynamic of truth and belief between Rat Kiley and Mitchell Sanders. The vignette begins with O'Brien talking about truth. Rat, the company believed, told a certain amount of truth in each of his stories, but always exaggerated them as well. They never disbelieved him, but never fully trusted his "facts." So it was with this story, which Sanders insists just does not "ring true."

Kiley, however, insists that he is a witness to most of the actual events. Slowly, as the story of Mary Anne's transformation progresses, Sanders focuses his objections less on the truth of Kiley's story and more on the telling itself. He and the other members of the troop pick out particular words like "dumb" and challenge Kiley on his exact characterization of Mary Anne. O'Brien comments on people's expectations about stories and their purpose in telling them. In the chapter, Kiley stops and asks Sanders what he thinks happened next in the story, challenging Sanders to share his expectations of stories. This action raises issues about the veracity of the story that Rat tells.

O'Brien talks about how Kiley tells the story, with a broken flow and interjecting his own thoughts into the meaning. Sanders takes up this side of storytelling, saying "the whole tone, man, you're wrecking it." Sanders has moved from not believing to believing so much that he wants the story told better. When Kiley admits he does not know what happened to Mary Anne, Sanders gets up-in-arms and says that telling a story without an ending violates the rules of storytelling. To Sanders, endings complete stories and make them true. He has now completely dissolved any difference between story and truth (or fiction and fact).

The meta-textual discussion of storytelling must be applied to author O'Brien. He tells a story with no ending, and his characters seem to know that. Perhaps that is why they are so troubled and why Sanders desperately wants an ending to Mary Anne's story. Sanders learns that however much truth there is to Kiley's story, he is more interested in the emotional weight of the tale, seeking completion. O'Brien successfully obscures the line between story and truth, and readers must ponder how much of the story is "true," how much is fictional, and whether that makes a difference in how we receive the novel.

The tale is about loss of innocence. Mary Anne is a convenient character because as a young person from the suburbs, a high school sweetheart, and a woman, she personifies innocence to the soldiers. Her progression from a sweet girlfriend to something more bestial than the Green Berets is an analogy for the loss of innocence through which all soldiers of Vietnam go. "O'Brien," Azar, Kiowa, Sanders, and all the young men sent to Vietnam departed from America "green" and left their innocence like baggage on the fields of a foreign land. For Mary Anne, the presence of her sweetheart gave her moments of pause in her transformation, where she took occasional steps back into sweetness. For the men of Alpha Company, a letter, a picture, or a pair of stockings could have pulled them back to the world of cleanliness and refinement, the world of love. Eventually, though, they all passed into the war, into violence, dirt, murder, and darkness. Just like Mary Anne, the innocent persons they were would never be seen again.

Sanders wants an ending to the story because he and the rest of the soldiers subconsciously want to know how their own lives will turn out. How will they return to their families, or will they ever return? These questions are a major inquiry in war literature, like Ernest Hemingway's *In Our Time,* and one of the major questions of O'Brien's novel. This same desire is what motivates "O'Brien" to write about his experiences in Vietnam and to author a writer's memoir. This yearning for completion, such as "O'Brien's" return trip to Vietnam in "Field Trip," is a major impetus in war novels in general, as a method of combating the general sense of meaninglessness that marks modern wars.

Glossary

culottes A woman's or girl's garment consisting of trousers made full in the legs to resemble a skirt.

rear-echelon A subdivision of a military force, farthest from the enemy.

NCO Noncommissioned officer.

E-6 An enlisted man's grade.

RFs, PFs Regional forces of S. Vietnam, also called Ruff-Puffs.

ARVN Army of the Republic of Vietnam (Army of S. Vietnam).

Green Beret A member of the Special Forces of the U.S. Army, the "Green Berets" (from the *green beret* worn as part of the uniform).

EM Enlisted man.

C-130 (Hercules) Aircraft that primarily performs the tactical portion of an airlift mission. It can operate from rough dirt strips and is the prime transport for airdropping troops and equipment into hostile areas.

USO United Service Organizations, a civilian arm of the U.S. Army that offered diversions and entertainment for soldiers both on the homefront and in active combat areas overseas.

hootch Military slang for a place to live in, specifically a shack or thatched hut, as in Vietnam.

Sterno Trademark for gelatinized methyl alcohol with nitrocellulose, sold in cans as a fuel for small stoves or chafing dishes.

ville A small village or group of huts in rural Vietnam.

AK-47 Basic infantry weapon of the NVA and Viet Cong.

Darvon A white, crystalline, narcotic analgesic used for the alleviation of moderate pain.

joss sticks Thin sticks of dried paste made of fragrant wood dust, a kind of incense.

MP Military Police.

CID Criminal Investigation Department.

Stockings

Summary

O'Brien recalls a fellow soldier, Henry Dobbins, and his habit of wrapping his girlfriend's pantyhose around his neck as a sort of "talisman," or lucky charm. O'Brien remembers Dobbins as a simple man with good intentions. When caught in a fight in the middle of an open field, Dobbins wrapped the pantyhose around his face and made it through the fight unscathed. The pantyhose, he believed, kept him safe, and he continued his eccentric practice even after his girlfriend broke up with him because he said the magic did not go away.

Commentary

The vignette is essentially a character sketch of Henry Dobbins. O'Brien devotes several of his chapters in *The Things They Carried* to such character sketches not only to create a vivid story but also to author a portrait of Vietnam that is more personal than political, more realistic than fantastic. From such chapters as "The Dentist" and "Stockings," we get to know the men and their idiosyncrasies, and O'Brien takes us through Vietnam with him rather than just reporting events and names.

In contrast to Curt Lemon, O'Brien's portrait of Henry Dobbins is a positive account of faith and hope. Dobbins is shown to be a strong man because he has faith. O'Brien outlines the many good parts of Dobbins and then complicates that by comparing him to America. Dobbins, O'Brien says, is like America in that both are "big and strong, full of good intentions, a roll of fat jiggling at his belly, slow of foot but always plodding along." The comparison starts well, and begins to wane to the point where we wonder whether O'Brien is criticizing America for being fat and slow or whether he has simply dropped the analogy. O'Brien shows Dobbins to be as the sons of America, exemplifying its great and dubious qualities alike, creating a realistic rather than jingoistic portrait of war and soldiers.

The main image in this vignette is the pair of stockings that Dobbins hangs around his neck. Stockings conjure up a number of meanings. First, there is some gender mixing when a man wears a woman's garment, demonstrating what we might now call a sexual fetish. Wrapping the stockings around his neck and pulling them over his nose, Dobbins displays a yearning for the feminine, gentler side of himself. Second, and most obviously, the stockings are a symbol of love and home. They are out of place in Vietnam where the soldiers have neither women nor refinement. Stockings recall memories of more pleasant times when Dobbins was with his girlfriend, away from the war and the jungle. So powerful are the stockings that they become a talisman, giving Dobbins real power to stay healthy and injury-free. Of course, we know that no nylon stockings would ever deflect bullets, but O'Brien shows how they affected a positive change of mind in Dobbins, and mental state affects reality. That is why O'Brien gives us so many stories where characters try to understand—the stockings give Dobbins an understanding, or a state of mind, that makes him more powerful.

Of course, in the end O'Brien robs us from this analysis by reporting that Dobbins's girlfriend breaks up with him, and Dobbins retains the stockings still. The power of the stockings, then, does not come from love or the memory of his girlfriend, but from Dobbins himself. They will continue to protect him so long as he believes in them. O'Brien shows us that anyone could have had stockings, whether Jensen's jackknife or Cross's picture. Anyone could have used anything as his own talisman. But Dobbins is singled out as someone who did. He found hope more than the other members of the company.

Glossary

bouncing Betty   An explosive that propels upward from the ground and then detonates.

Church

Summary

One afternoon the unit comes across a pagoda where two monks who speak little English live in a shack. One monk leads the men into the rundown pagoda where they spend the night and set up a base of operations. The monks take pride in offering the men small items like a chair and watermelons. The monks especially like Henry Dobbins and learn to help him clean his machine gun.

Dobbins tells Kiowa that he might join up with these monks after the war. He explains that he is not interested in the scholarly aspects of religion, but that he would enjoy being nice to people. Kiowa says that he would not want to be a minister but that he likes church, and he repeats that he feels wrong about setting up camp in the pagoda.

Commentary

In this vignette, O'Brien introduces a church, a site of religion and solemnity, into the daily affairs of war. Through Kiowa and Dobbins, O'Brien contrasts the church with the Vietnam country and the monks with the soldiers. The church and the monks stand outside of the war experience of Vietnam and the company of soldiers, but the two worlds come together when the church is used as a base of operations. Like the "Style" vignette later in the book, the soldiers watch the movements of the natives without understanding either language or meaning. In order to understand them or to arrive at any sort of meaning for the war for themselves, the soldiers can only imitate the language, movements, and habits of the monks and hope it will increase their sensitivity and diminish their dismissive and discriminatory attitude toward others unlike themselves.

Character Insight

Dobbins again is the central character, and as he reveals to Kiowa that he harbors an inclination to become a religious leader of some sort, he is able to make a stronger connection to the monks than the rest of the troops. He respects and understands the choice they have made because of a desire deep within him, a remnant from his childhood. Without being able to understand the language or the meaning of the "strange washing motion" of the monks, Dobbins and the monks establish a special liking for one another. They call him "good soldier Jesus," using very simple English words that they know to describe what they know of him: He is good, he is a soldier, and he is a Christian. Dobbins does not understand all of them either, but teaches them to clean his rifle, showing them trust and respect. He also imagines them to be what he cannot ever know: kind and intelligent. He derides his own intellect by believing he would make a good people person but lack the brains and religious faith of a minister, and under it he assumes that these monks have all of those qualities. Dobbins interprets their silence as kindness, faith, and intelligence, assuming the best about them though he has no reason to believe this.

As the conversation between Kiowa and Dobbins progresses, both feel a growing respect for the calm solemnity of a church, culminating in Kiowa's statement, "This is all wrong." The soldiers have interlaced the war with the church, and that violates what both Kiowa and Dobbins believe should be. In the end, Dobbins respectfully dismisses the monks in their own language, making an effort to bridge the gap between them from his side, and imitates the hand washing motion of the monks. He does not understand it yet, but tries to mimic the action and give some meaning to the monks (and to himself) outside of his grasp. Like the dancer in "Style," the soldier can only copy the movements without any real understanding. For Dobbins, it is an important gesture—he understands that they have been wrong, and he is trying to do all that he can to make amends.

Glossary

pagoda In India and the Far East, a temple in the form of a pyramidal tower of several stories, usually an odd number, commonly built over a sacred relic or as a work of devotion.

Friar Tuck The religious leader of Robin Hood's gang of Merry Men, from the English folk tale, *Robin Hood*.

di di mau A Vietnamese phrase meaning to move quickly.

The Man I Killed/
Ambush

Summary

O'Brien describes a Viet Cong soldier whom he has killed, using meticulous physical detail, including descriptions of his wounds. Then O'Brien imagines the life story of this man and imagines that he was a scholar who felt an obligation to defend his village.

Azar comments to O'Brien about the dead soldier and is sent away by Kiowa, who senses that O'Brien is upset. Kiowa tells O'Brien to stop staring at the body and offers justifications for what has happened. O'Brien continues to imagine that the man he killed was devoted to his studies, that he wrote poems, and that he fell in love with his classmate. O'Brien sees that the man's fingernails and hair are clean and guesses that he has been a soldier for only one day. Later Kiowa tells O'Brien that he is looking better; even later he tells O'Brien that he should talk about it, and again tries to get the disturbed O'Brien to talk.

O'Brien's daughter, Kathleen, asked him when she was nine years old if he had ever killed anyone. He told her no, but hopes that she will ask again as an adult. Again, O'Brien describes the Viet Cong soldier and tells how he saw him approach through the morning fog. He recalls being terrified, and that his action was automatic, not political and not personal. He believes, too, that if he had not thrown the grenade, the Vietnamese soldier would have passed by without incident.

Commentary

The central theme of this vignette is time. "O'Brien" the soldier is frozen in a moment in time, recalling the entire history of the dead Vietnamese man while the American troop of soldiers are all moving forward, preparing for another day at war. The one word that best describes the mood of this vignette is shock. "O'Brien" is in shock from killing the man, and the rest of the world is moving around him, all in speech and imagination.

**Style &
Language**

O'Brien has his two American comrades, Azar and Kiowa, try to move around "O'Brien." Azar sees only a fallen enemy and compliments "O'Brien" on a thorough job—he cannot understand what "O'Brien" is feeling. Kiowa is more sympathetic, offering textbook comments, such as switching places with the dead man and that he would have been killed anyway, in order to console "O'Brien" whom he believes regrets his action. The fact is that "O'Brien" never expresses what he is feeling—joy, regret, pain, confusion, or any specific emotion. He never says a word throughout the story. His shock is all that we can really know, expressed through his silence.

Much of this vignette is full of the personal history of the Vietnamese soldier, beginning with his birthplace, moving through his career, love life, and eventual enlisting in the army. It also details some of his hopes and ambitions. O'Brien uses this history to make the dead man more realistic—the audience cannot simply dismiss him as a body or an enemy, but must think of him as a man. This is yet another way O'Brien makes the Vietnam War more personal than historical or political.

Theme

On the other hand, the history of the dead Vietnamese soldier is fictional. We know that there is no way that "O'Brien" could know all that he thinks, or even most of it. O'Brien is again playing with the notion of truth: The personal history makes the soldier truer to us, more of a real person, but none of what "O'Brien" expresses is necessarily fact. The truth of the fallen soldier is left up to the reader. We can decide whether we feel for this man or want to think of him only as a fallen enemy.

The main image in this story is the star-shaped wound. It is repeated several times throughout the vignette. The star might symbolize hope, like a wishing star, but O'Brien has inverted its meaning by tying it in with death. It is surely no coincidence that the star-shaped wound is on the soldier's eye, for it is with the eyes that men both gaze upon the stars and see the approaching enemy. The Vietnamese soldier obviously did not see the danger he was in; perhaps he was gazing more upon the stars, upon his future, than on his present situation. In this case, the stars betrayed him, and he has no future. In this story, O'Brien changes the meaning of looking to the future and the hopefulness of the star through his use of this image.

The "Ambush" vignette collapses all time between the experience of "O'Brien" in Vietnam and O'Brien the author telling a story. There are three distinct points of time referred to in the vignette: the time when his daughter, as a child, asked him the question about killing a man; the time that the author is telling his story; and the time of the story itself, some twenty years earlier in Vietnam. For the author, though, any perspective that he now has is lost in the telling of the tale, and the confusion and fear that he felt as a soldier then is intimately entangled with the regret and embarrassment he now feels through reflection. He is as unsure now as then, and even though he acted more out of instinct when he lobbed the grenade and insists that he did not ponder "morality or politics or military duty," his reevaluation now forces O'Brien to reckon his action against those gauges.

Character Insight

This story, perhaps more vividly than most of the novel, puts us in the mind and body of "O'Brien" the soldier. We see through his eyes and share his thoughts. Much of what O'Brien describes is formulaic, such as not feeling hate, acting on instinct, feelings of regret afterwards, and moral confusion that lingers. What is unique about O'Brien's treatment of this killing is how he introduces his daughter into the equation. Instead of a man reflecting and reconciling his actions to himself, he now has to justify them to a new audience—one who looks to him for moral guidance. His response is to lie to her and to wait until writing this vignette to undo that lie. O'Brien gives no indication that he has ever lied to himself about what happened. Even immediately after the killing, when Kiowa tries to convince him that he did nothing wrong, "O'Brien" insists that "none of it mattered." He focused only on the body, on the physical damage done, not the moral implications.

So, competing in this vignette are O'Brien's desires to understand his own actions and his need to relate them to his daughter, as well as move beyond what he did. The final image of the soon-to-be dead soldier walking toward O'Brien and smiling is an act of revenge. The dead soldier not only lingers in O'Brien's thoughts, but also seems to enjoy that O'Brien cannot finish "sorting it out." We never know if O'Brien is seeking forgiveness or if he thinks he needs it, but whatever will not leave him is what kept him from answering his daughter truthfully. Perhaps that itself is what makes him write the story, searching for some kind of closure to either his killing or his lying.

Glossary

Trung sisters   (d. 42 C.E.) Trung Trac and Trung Nhi, were daughters of a powerful Vietnamese lord who lived at the beginning of the first century.

Tran Hung Dao   Famous general who defeated two Mongol invasions in late thirteenth-century Vietnam.

Tot Dong   Field in 1426 where the Vietnamese routed the Chinese. Two years later, the Chinese recognized Vietnam's independence.

48th Viet Cong Battalion   One of the most effective Viet Cong military units.

Style

Summary

A Vietnamese girl seems to be dancing among the ruins of a burnt-out hamlet. Her house has burned down and her family killed, yet she continues to move and dance despite the devastation she sees, her face quiet and composed. Later that night, Azar mocks and mimics the girl's gestures. Henry Dobbins disapproves and threatens him to make him stop if he does not dance right.

Commentary

The central symbol in this vignette is the dance of the young girl. The characters understand dancing as deliberate, purposeful, graceful, and meaningful: everything that the war in Vietnam is not. The repeating theme is that the characters labor to understand why the girl is dancing and the meaning of her dance. All around lies destruction, decay, and death, and yet she dances. Perhaps she dances as an escape from her reality; perhaps she dances to deny her reality; or perhaps, as Azar says, she dances a ritual that gives meaning to what has happened. When she covers her ears with her hands, she may be either blocking out sound or acting out an ornate cultural ritual.

Regardless of the meaning of the dance, O'Brien makes it clear that the American soldiers do not understand either why she dances or what the dance means. To them, this scene is one of destruction and the dancing girl is an abomination. Everything else fits the schema of destruction and war, the dance alone stands out. And yet it is around her dance that the story revolves and the soldiers continually lead their discussion. To them, there must be meaning, and meaning is what they desperately lack.

In fact, the dancing girl is one of the most optimistic symbols O'Brien gives us in the novel, for clearly she symbolizes something, even if we cannot know it. The soldiers cannot ignore her because they are starving for meaning in their campaign; any meaning, even the meaning of a small girl dancing in the middle of dead bodies and ashes. She pays them and their doings no heed, and yet they constantly attend her dance, seeking its meaning.

Style & Language

O'Brien deliberately uses open words when he says that later that night "Azar mocked the girl's dancing." On the one hand, Azar could just have been imitating the dance; on the other hand, he may also have been making light of it, the pejorative meaning of "mock." But this haunting statement is only a smokescreen: O'Brien is tricking us and wondering whether we will catch the main point—that Azar is now dancing. Even after they have left the scene and the girl behind, their minds still dwell on the dance and its elusive meaning. For the soldiers, if they can do the dance properly, they may understand something, anything about where they are and what they are doing there.

In the end, the pseudo-hero of the vignette, Henry Dobbins, proves to be the most deluded. He stops Azar from dancing and warns him that he should dance "right." What Dobbins does not understand, and what is unspeakably beyond the comprehension of the band of soldiers, is that they cannot dance right, for they have no meaning to deliver. All they can do is make large dance-like gestures, mocking what they cannot, but what they desperately want to, understand.

Speaking of Courage

Summary

After his service in the Vietnam War, Norman Bowker returns home and has difficulty adjusting to the normalcy of everyday life. In the late afternoon on the Fourth of July holiday, Norman drives around a local lake, passing time and thinking about his life before the war, as well as what he saw and did in Vietnam. He recalls driving around the lake with Sally before the war and remembers how a childhood friend drowned in the lake. He thinks about how his friends have gotten married or moved away to find jobs.

Norman wants to talk about Vietnam, and he imagines how he would tell his father about almost earning a Silver Star, but his father is too busy to listen. Norman wants to talk about nearly saving Kiowa's life and about how he feels he failed in not doing so. He contemplates telling his stories about Vietnam to four railway workers he sees.

As Norman continues to drive around the lake, he listens to the radio and thinks more about bravery. He thinks about how he would explain the incidents that led up to Kiowa's death and recalls the scene with great detail as the memories play again and again in his mind like a movie. Later, he pulls into an A&W drive-in restaurant and tries to place an order with the carhop, who tells him to talk into the intercom. After he finishes eating, he presses the intercom button again and begins to tell his story to the voice at the other end of the intercom, but he changes his mind and resumes his drive around the lake. Later he stops and watches the fireworks show.

Commentary

Literary
Device

Of the characters O'Brien revisits in a post-war story, Norman Bowker is by far the one who has the most difficult time carrying—to draw on the metaphor O'Brien presents in the novel's title—the burden of memory. It is important to note that, like the first chapter, this chapter is told by a third person narrator—the narrator "O'Brien" is largely absent from this chapter as a witness or commentator, though he comments on it in the chapter that follows. Instead, O'Brien employs a stream-of-consciousness technique that allows readers to learn the details of Kiowa's death by "overhearing" Bowker's interior dialogue.

Norman's problem is one of not having an audience to which he can address the stories of Vietnam that weigh heavily on him emotionally. O'Brien underscores Bowker's hesitation to tell others about his experiences in Vietnam, as he believes that they don't want to hear them. He imagines that his former girlfriend Sally's response would be one of horrified disapproval of the vulgarities of war, of the vulgarity of Kiowa's death in the shit field. He imagines that his father will be disinterested, thinking that he has his own World War II stories and that he would call Norman's courage and valor into question. This rejection by his father that he assumes will occur, combined with his sense that the "town seemed remote" and that "he felt invisible," contributes to the extreme alienation Norman feels.

O'Brien demonstrates this sense of disconnectedness and alienation through the *pathos* of Norman trying to tell his story, which he has a deep need and desire to do, but then becoming quiet again and keeping the story to himself, first with the men working, then with the boys he passes, and finally with the order taker at A&W. Norman's drive around the lake is a metaphor for this cycle of trying to articulate his story; he circles the familiar town where he grew up looking for his place in it, looking for what he should do next with his life, but being unable to discover that answer. Similarly, he needs to tell his story to begin to come to terms with and take meaning from the memories of Vietnam that creep into his thoughts. Norman, then, is searching for meaning. Norman's repetitive drive in circles around the lake recalls the dancing girl that the troop encounters in "Style;" both are acting out a search for meaning.

Before Norman can tell his story or find meaning, he must resolve the conflict between fear and courage that is at the core of his story of Kiowa's death. The elusive Silver Star is a symbol with its meanings in conflict within the context of this chapter: The award is a military recognition of valor, but Norman would have won it for an act that seems somehow incongruous, saving Kiowa from drowning in the muddy field of human excrement. Because of this incongruity, Norman cannot tell the whole story. He imagines that his father, a veteran himself who understands medals as inaccurate measures of heroism ("knowing full well that many brave men do not win medals for their bravery, and that others win medals for doing nothing") might ask him about the Silver Star. In answering his father's inquiry, Norman would first describe in detail the seven medals he had been awarded. Next he would begin to describe the river, though he would omit that they had mistakenly set up camp in the village's area for excrement. Finally he would ask, "You really want to hear this?" and then continue until he remembers the smell, and his ability to tell the story fails. As Norman's narration breaks off, he notices people and activity around the lake, and he starts another turn around the lake. He goes around and around the lake, which also has an offensive and stinking smell, but does not move to it, as he does not get to the shit field in his story as he tells it to his father in his imagination.

Theme

This inability to tell the complete story, shit and all, is linked to the conflict between memory and nostalgia in the chapter. O'Brien deliberately chooses to set the story on the Fourth of July, which creates a counterpoint between cliché conceptions of patriotism and heroism and the reality of what war demands from those who participate in it. As Norman continues to play out the scenario in his mind about telling the story of the shit field, it becomes clear to him that he cannot tell the crux of the story, his attempt to save Kiowa from drowning: "He could not describe what happened next, not ever, but he would've tried anyway." This inability recalls "O'Brien's" admission in "On the Rainy River," also a story about courage, that he had never told that story before. Their shared inability is related to a sense of shame and embarrassment that both men carry, O'Brien for going to war and Norman for choosing to live, releasing Kiowa's boot and thinking, "Not here...Not like this."

After his eleventh revolution around the lake, Norman thinks about telling his father that "the truth is that I let [Kiowa] go." His father's response, one dismissive of the death but praising of Norman's other seven medals, indicates that he has missed the entire truth of the story, which is his son's desperate sense of guilt. Norman cannot even get that far in telling his story; he cannot tell the story because survivors and witnesses tell the stories that become history. Through his symbolic wading into the lake and putting his head under and tasting the water, readers understand that Bowker sort of died in Vietnam and cannot recover because he cannot find meaning in his life after the war.

Glossary

Silver Star   A U.S. military decoration in the form of a bronze star with a small silver star at the center, awarded for gallantry in action.

Combat Infantryman's Badge   An award designed for enlisted men and below who have served in active combat zones.

Air Medal   A U.S. military decoration awarded for meritorious achievement during participation in aerial operations.

Army Commendation Medal   Awarded to any member of the Armed Forces of the U.S., other than general officers, who, while serving in any capacity after December 6, 1941, distinguished himself by heroism, meritorious achievement or meritorious service.

Good Conduct Medal   A U.S. military decoration awarded for exemplary behavior, efficiency, and fidelity.

Vietnam Campaign Medal   Awarded to personnel who meet one of the following requirements: (1) served in Vietnam for six months during the period of March 1, 1961 and March 28, 1973, (2) served outside Vietnam and contributed direct combat support to Vietnam and Armed Forces for six months, or (3) six months service is not required for individuals who were wounded by hostile forces; killed in action or otherwise in line of duty; or captured by hostile forces.

ribbons   Strips of cloth, often of many colors, worn on the left breast of a military uniform to indicate an award of a decoration or medal.

bivouacked   Encamped in the open, with only tents or improvised shelter.

shrapnel   Any fragments scattered by an exploding shell or bomb.

carhop   A waiter or, especially, a waitress who serves food to customers in cars at a drive-in restaurant.

the Y   Abbreviation for the Young Men's Christian Association. A social center for recreational activities.

seven honeys   Seven medals.

Notes

Summary

O'Brien discusses the preceding chapter, "Speaking of Courage," and tells the supposedly "true story" behind the fictional story. Bowker, who hanged himself three years after the story was written, suggested to O'Brien that he write the story. In spring 1975, O'Brien received a letter from Bowker describing his struggle to find a meaningful use of his life. Bowker had dropped out of community college and instead spent his mornings in bed, his afternoons playing pickup games of basketball, and his nights driving around aimlessly. O'Brien excerpts long passages of Bowker's letter, which suggested that O'Brien should write a story about a veteran who feels like he died in Vietnam and cannot adjust to daily life.

O'Brien comments on the letter and himself and how it seemed to him that he had a remarkably easy time adjusting to life after the war. He realizes that he has in fact been talking about the war through his writing, and comments that the act of telling stories allows people to objectify their experiences and maybe cope with them a bit more easily.

O'Brien then explains how he tried to work the material of Norman Bowker's story into a different novel, which forced him to omit some elements of the "true" story. This version was published as a short story, which Norman read and felt was terrible.

A few years later, O'Brien received a note from Norman's mother explaining that her son committed suicide. O'Brien clarifies that Norman was not responsible for Kiowa's death, and that the Silver Star portion of the story is made up.

Commentary

"Notes" is the key vignette for unlocking the medium-is-the-message form of O'Brien's novel. Just as the title indicates, in this chapter "O'Brien" offers commentary, or notes, on how the preceding chapter, and more generally, the novel, was conceived and shaped into its final form. Again O'Brien returns to the novel's overarching theme of the relation between fact and fiction and the "truthfulness" inherent in stories that are not necessarily "actual" or "factual."

Though readers can easily mistake the protagonist "Tim O'Brien" for the actual novelist, readers must keep this divide in mind to fully understand this chapter, or the novel as a whole. The most important aspect of the chapter is the description of the process through which the fictional "O'Brien," a middle-aged writer, turns the stuff of memory into stories. In so doing, O'Brien collapses boundaries between the two genres that *The Things They Carried* occupies: the ("fictional") war autobiography of "Tim O'Brien" and the ("fictional") writer's memoir of "Tim O'Brien."

Theme

By walking the reader through the genesis of "Speaking of Courage," O'Brien more thoroughly comments on the running thread of the theme of storytelling. The protagonist "O'Brien" compares himself to Norman Bowker, commenting that he, too, rarely spoke of the war, but that he "had been talking about it virtually non-stop through [his] writing." His writing was a way to issue meaning to the random events that had occurred to him, an ability that Norman Bowker badly needed but did not possess. Bowker looked to "O'Brien" to articulate the feeling of loss that Kiowa's death brought him. "O'Brien's" multiple versions of the story of Kiowa's death stand in contrast to Bowker's; Bowker's is an extremely subjective account, one which claims vast culpability and has the dire result of suicide, the ultimate subjective act. On the other hand, O'Brien outlines the usefulness of storytelling because it allows "you to objectify your own experience." This storytelling ability is exactly what Norman Bowker is incapable of, and also what affords "O'Brien" the vantage, first, to tell the story Norman cannot and, second, to use that story to better understand himself. O'Brien achieves this by describing the landscape "O'Brien" placed in the "Speaking of Courage" vignette: "O'Brien" transplants the details of his native Minnesota to Norman Bowker's Iowa.

As "O'Brien" attempted to wedge the story into *Going After Cacciato,* incidentally a novel by Tim O'Brien, he realized that its artifice made the story a failure, particularly when paired with his fear to "speak directly" by confronting his memories of the night in the shit field. Norman, with his highly sensitive personalized stake in the story, immediately recognized the story's failure: The night in the shit field had not been truly "objectified" so that it could be understood; rather, O'Brien had avoided the important details of the event because he feared them.

As with most of O'Brien's stories, this one, too, is symbolic on a meta-textual level. Finally, "O'Brien" tells the reader that his objective in "Speaking of Courage" is to make good on Norman's silence, which—despite the sometimes unreliable narrator—it does. The reader can also make this connection for "O'Brien," that he makes good on his silence, and can extend the trope of the usefulness of storytelling to "Speaking of Courage" itself. The story, which does make good on Norman Bowker's silence, does doubly so, because the exercise of writing saves "Tim O'Brien" from a similar fate.

Glossary

Saigon's final collapse   April 30, 1975, Saigon fell to the North Vietnamese Army, effectively the end of the Vietnam War.

If I Die in a Combat Zone   Novel by O'Brien in which he recounts what it was like to be a foot soldier during the Vietnam War: from his induction in Minnesota, to the horrors of boot camp, to the daily terrors of the Vietnam jungles.

flashback   A vivid, spontaneous recollection of a past experience.

Going After Cacciato   Novel by O'Brien in which a private deserts his post in Vietnam, intent on walking 8,000 miles to Paris for the peace talks. The remaining members of his squad are sent after him.

In the Field

Summary

The morning after Kiowa's death, the platoon searches the area for his body. Lt. Cross watches his men as they search and thinks about the impact of Kiowa's death. Azar makes jokes about the style of Kiowa's death, but Bowker warns him to stop. Mitchell Sanders and Norman Bowker eventually recover Kiowa's rucksack, and they argue over who is responsible for Kiowa's death; Sanders blames Lt. Cross, but Bowker disagrees. Meanwhile, Lt. Cross rehearses a letter he might write to Kiowa's father, but his thoughts wander back to his own culpability because he chose that particular field on which to camp. Lt. Cross wades across the field to a soldier who is shaking and sobbing. The young soldier is sorry because he thinks he may have caused Kiowa's death by accidentally signaling their presence to the enemy by switching on a flashlight. The soldier is searching for a photo of his girlfriend, and Lt. Cross feels pity for him.

Norman Bowker locates the corpse, and Mitchell Sanders warns Azar not to make any more jokes or crude comments. They finally dislodge the body from the muddy bottom of the field and are saddened and relieved, but they also felt a secret joy because they are alive. Azar feels some guilt over his earlier jokes.

Lt. Cross lets himself sink into the mud and floats while he revises the letter to Kiowa's father in his mind. The upset soldier tries to confess his guilt to Lt. Cross, who does not listen, escaping the scene by remembering his life before the war.

Commentary

Style & Language

This vignette is one of the more depressing in the book, one where O'Brien makes it impossible to think about the Vietnam War as a whole. Instead, he forces us to look at the war person by person. The entire event of searching for Kiowa's body is like a break from the political war—something that men do for their friends rather than for their country. The three centers in the story, Lt. Cross, the young, nameless soldier, and the rest of the troop searching for Kiowa's body each have their own perspective. This vignette is a compilation of their perspectives, not a story with facts and details.

Lt. Cross is laden with guilt, not only as a commander but also as someone who feels personally responsible for Kiowa's death. As a matter of protocol, he is responsible because he ordered the camp to be made, but Cross feels his responsibility and remorse more deeply than his duty dictates. Although O'Brien tells us about how Cross does not desire to command, Cross himself focuses on Kiowa's father and the letter that he must now write. To Cross, Kiowa's death personalizes his fears and his responsibility not just to care for his men, but that he must answer for them to others—like fathers, commanders, and even God.

The men searching for Kiowa's body are themselves upset and terrified. As they wade through a river of excrement, searching for a friend and soldier, they feel respect and awe. Azar's jokes about irony and death bother Bowker because of his feelings about the tragic death of his friend and comrade, but also because of a sharpened awareness of his own mortality. When they uncover the body, Azar himself feels these same forces, but he needed the reality of a corpse to drive it home. Until then, he felt more invincible. But Kiowa's death means that his luck ran out, and luck could run out for any of them at any time.

Theme

O'Brien never suggests that a soldier stayed alive because of skill or prowess, but rather because of his luck. Luck, which seems to be rationed out like food to soldiers, was a man's to use or expend, and Kiowa's had run out. This does not make Kiowa's death less tragic, but more universal. It could happen to any of them. There is no way to measure luck—it is a random element in war that they all depended upon but which none of them could control.

Finally, there is the young soldier who is not named. He has no name because he is no one in particular, just any soldier who could have made a simple mistake and caused his own or someone else's death. He is, of course, filled with guilt and sees Kiowa's death as his personal fault, just as Cross does. They both believe that "when a man died, there had to be blame." In fact, O'Brien shows us that there is no blame because there is no reason. Perhaps the flashlight signaled the enemy as to their position, but the rest of the soldiers know that it was just bad luck. The Viet Cong soldier killed by "O'Brien" was killed because his luck had run out, nothing more than wandering down the wrong path at the wrong time. The nameless soldier does not understand this, and it is so terrifying an idea that he cannot think it. Instead, he searches for the lost picture of a past girlfriend, needing something he knows and trusts. Reality, randomness, luck, and war are too much for both Cross and the boy.

Glossary

MIA   Missing in action. A person in the armed forces who is lost during combat and who cannot be accounted for as a known casualty.

GI   Member of the U.S. armed forces; especially an enlisted soldier.

Karl (Heinrich) Marx   (1818–1883) German social philosopher and economist. Marx was the founder of modern socialism.

Good Form

Summary

O'Brien explains that he is a writer now and was once a soldier, but that most of the other stories comprising his "memoir" are invented and that he never killed the Viet Cong soldier. He explains that his style of stories that seem to be truthful but are fiction demonstrate that "story-truth is truer sometimes than happening-truth." O'Brien, as an author, explains that stories can be used to tell the truth or a version of it, like when Kathleen asks O'Brien if he has ever killed a man and he says yes.

Commentary

Author Tim O'Brien reminds his readers that the protagonist of the novel is a writer, an individual whose job it is to meld memory and imagination into a new product for others to derive meaning from. O'Brien has melded these elements and created an innovative form for the novel that combines his own experiences—he is a Vietnam veteran—and his ability as a fiction writer to animate fragments of memory through embellishment and invention. In other words, O'Brien uses the "real" as a point of departure for his storytelling because he believes that imagined accounts could have legitimate kernels of truth.

As in "How to Tell a True War Story," O'Brien reprises differentiating between, as "O'Brien" puts it, "story-truth" and "happening truth." "O'Brien" bluntly states his objective as an author: "I want you to feel what I felt," which underpins and justifies "O'Brien's" major admission in the chapter: "I did not kill him."

Finally, "O'Brien" comments on the temporal aspect of stories, how—even if the details are fabricated—they "make things present." Included in those "things" are "things ['O'Brien'] never looked at." Just as "O'Brien" looked away from the dead Vietnamese man in "The Lives of the Dead" when he was "actually" in Vietnam, "actually" right in front of the corpse, only in his mind—at the intersection where the past meets the present—does he make sense of it. This explains the post-modern paradox that closes the chapter: O'Brien's assertion that he will be able to answer "yes" if his daughter asks whether he has ever killed a man and to answer honestly "of course not." This recalls the scene in "Ambush" when O'Brien hopes that his daughter will one day, as an adult, ask again about his involvement in the war. This also recalls Kathleen's question at the close of "Field Trip" when she asks whether the Vietnamese farmers are still angry. Meaning, then, O'Brien suggests, shifts with time, and the main variable is when the past melds with the present in the mind of the storyteller. O'Brien can answer "yes" or "of course not" because, as the novel demonstrates, O'Brien has constructed and deconstructed these scenarios and internalized their meanings.

Field Trip

Summary

O'Brien and his daughter travel to Vietnam and visit the site of Kiowa's death. O'Brien and 10-year-old Kathleen visit the tourist spots, which she enjoys, but it is clear to him that she does not understand the war that had happened 20 years earlier. She wonders "why was everybody so mad at everybody else." She thinks her father is "weird" because he cannot forget the past.

They arrive at the field where Kiowa died, and O'Brien notes how it looks like any farming field now. They walk to where the field meets the river. O'Brien unwraps a cloth bundle that holds Kiowa's old moccasins. With the moccasins, he wades in, swimming out to where Kiowa's rucksack had been recovered, and reaches in and wedges the moccasins into the river bottom. O'Brien holds the glance of an old Vietnamese farmer working nearby, whom Kathleen thinks looks angry. The man holds a shovel over his head like a flag, and O'Brien tells his daughter that the anger that the man would have felt was finished and in the past.

Commentary

The point of this vignette is for O'Brien to attain some closure for the loss of Kiowa. He held an image in his mind for over 20 years of the field where Kiowa had died, but he immediately finds that the reality is nothing like the image in his mind. For example, now the land seems to be at peace, where before every hill and blade of grass made him feel fear at night—the fear of war. Neither his memory nor his field trip were truer than the other—they were simply different truths. O'Brien questions what is Vietnam: Is it a memory, is it a country, is it both, or is it neither?

Not insignificantly, O'Brien brings his daughter, Kathleen, on this trip, for he wants her to understand more about his past. Yet he finds that as attentive and interested as she is, she does not understand much, like the need to trek out into one of a thousand fields in the middle of a foreign country. When she asks about the meaning, all O'Brien can do is give an obscure answer. At first he says that there are three different perspectives, Kathleen's, his own, and those who sent him to this country. In the end, though, he simply answers, "I don't know." It is not that Vietnam has no meaning, but that he cannot understand or explain it to anyone else, even his own daughter.

Kathleen does not see the need to remember; she calls her father "weird" for his inability to forget that past. O'Brien does not see himself as weird, however, and although he never says it, he must regret his daughter's immediate desire to ignore such an important piece of his past. Perhaps this is why when they are in the field, he does not make an exhaustive effort to explain everything to her.

Theme

The scene in the field is the climax of the story, where for once the production of meaning comes from O'Brien rather than simply having meaning swarm around him. He describes the field as the locus for his emotional emptiness; he blames it for the man he has become. It is in this field, however, that he is finally able to create meaning for some part of what happened to him. Unlike the dancing girl from "Style" and the unintelligible monks from "Church," this time it is O'Brien, wading out into the marsh, touching the water, who is participating in an action that has a meaning. Conversely, Kathleen is now the observer who can merely look upon her father and not understand what he is doing. So O'Brien the writer creates a cycle where meaning and ignorance move through a generation. Now he as an ex-soldier, a friend, a father, and also a writer will tell stories and give meaning. His audience, however, may not understand him, and maybe be left only to mock his movements rather than participate and communicate with him. O'Brien's battle has shifted from a field in Vietnam to a culture, and rather than a gun or knife he now has a story, a book, and a family with which he must contend.

Glossary

Ho Chi Minh's mausoleum Burial place of Ho Chi Minh, Vietnamese leader and first president of North Vietnam (1954–1969). His army was victorious in the French Indochina War (1946–1954), and he later led North Vietnam's struggle to defeat the U.S.-supported government in South Vietnam.

The Ghost Soldiers

Summary

O'Brien recalls the two times he was shot in Vietnam. The first time, medic Rat Kiley gave him medical care in the midst of battle, checking on him four times, finally helping O'Brien to a helicopter for evacuation to a hospital. O'Brien recuperated and returned to his unit nearly a month later and found that Rat had been wounded and replaced by a new medic named Bobby Jorgenson.

O'Brien was shot a second time, and he nearly died of shock before Jorgenson administered medical care. O'Brien felt intense anger toward Jorgenson. The wound developed gangrene, and O'Brien could not walk or sit. He felt humiliation and embarrassment and began planning ways to get even with Jorgenson.

After his release from the hospital, O'Brien was transferred out of combat to a supply restocking area, and he missed the feeling of fraternity that came from fighting alongside his friends. He continued to suffer pain from his wound.

Later his former company comes to his base for a stand-down, or break from combat duties. O'Brien greets Sanders, Azar, Henry Dobbins, Dave Jensen, and Norman Bowker, and spends the evening drinking and talking with them. He begins to realize that he is no longer a member of their intimate group and becomes jealous of the friendships from which he is now excluded.

O'Brien asks the others about Bobby Jorgenson. He obsesses over seeing Jorgenson, who is also on stand-down, but Mitchell Sanders advises him to give up because Bobby Jorgenson has learned how to be an excellent medic and has been accepted by the group of soldiers. O'Brien feels betrayed and becomes angry.

The next morning, Jorgenson waits for O'Brien because he wants to talk to him. Jorgenson apologizes, explaining that he didn't help O'Brien because he was paralyzed by fear. O'Brien does not fully accept the apology and decides to take revenge. After being rejected by Sanders, he partners with Azar to pull a prank on Jorgenson to scare him. He later considers canceling his "game" but sees Jorgenson with his old friends and decides to follow through.

O'Brien knows Jorgenson had night duty and plans to spook Jorgenson after dark. Azar and O'Brien string ropes attached to homemade noisemakers and tug the ropes to make frightening sounds in the darkness. O'Brien imagines Jorgenson trying to convince himself that there is no reason to be scared. He feels cruel, but he also laughs and feels powerful. As O'Brien and Azar prepare for the last of their tricks, O'Brien remembers getting shot and recalls his out-of-body experience. He wishes he could stop the prank but Azar takes over. Azar continues rattling the noisemakers and manipulating a contraption made of a sandbag to look like a ghost. Jorgenson shoots the sandbag and, realizing the prank, screams out O'Brien's name. Jorgenson tells O'Brien that he is pathetic; Azar agrees with Jorgenson and kicks O'Brien in the head. Jorgenson treats the gash on O'Brien's forehead, and they decide that they are now even.

Commentary

This story questions not only what we as readers think about the Vietnam War but also what those fighting in it believed. In this vignette, "O'Brien" gets wounded twice and is taken away from the fighting to serve in a battalion supply company, a transfer that he discovers tears him away from what he knew as Vietnam. The story revolves around the character of Bobby Jorgenson, but Jorgenson serves as a tool for O'Brien to illustrate important lessons of war and friendship.

Style & Language

Like many of O'Brien's stories, the most important pieces of this vignette are set at night. It is roaming around at night that "O'Brien" feels the sharpest pangs of hatred and yearnings for revenge against Jorgenson, it is at night that he hangs out with his old company and discovers how things have changed, and it is at night that he enacts his revenge against Jorgenson. This vignette and the following one, "Night Life," both deal with how the night affects people. To O'Brien, the world is different at night: The stifling darkness is maddening and intoxicating, able to confuse and enliven a soldier. It is at night that Vietnam comes alive—not the country as much as the experience of being a soldier. In this story, "O'Brien" must act at night in order to be like a soldier again against Jorgenson.

O'Brien lets us either forgive the mistakes Jorgenson makes treating "O'Brien" or not. Jorgenson's character is introduced as "green" specifically so that we can excuse him, which the other members of Alpha Company do later on. Regardless of whether we agree with "O'Brien" retaining so much anger, it is clear that he feels embarrassment and humiliation from his getting wounded, leading to pent-up resentment and hostility all focused on Jorgenson. Of course, "O'Brien" is also dealing with the loss of his life as a combat soldier—he missed the adventure, brotherhood, and feeling of being "awake" that can only come when the "presence of death" is always a looming danger. (O'Brien also challenges this idea by saying that death is also a possibility at a baseball game, again emphasizing the randomness of war.) "O'Brien" admits that he misses his company, whom he considers "close friends," and all of these feelings of loss are converted into anger toward Jorgenson. O'Brien emphasizes many of the common feelings that combat veterans express, especially the togetherness and close friendships that a tour of combat duty bring. He also challenges those ideas in this story by having "O'Brien" meet up again with his old company.

When Alpha Company arrives on "O'Brien's" base, he quickly realizes that his situation has changed. When his anger toward Jorgenson comes up, his "friends" step up to defend Jorgenson as a member of their team. Sanders' line, "...Jorgenson—he's *with* us now," shows O'Brien that he is no longer a part of the team, and the loyalty and friendship he assumed existed between all of them was more tenuous than he had imagined. O'Brien realizes that loyalty and allegiance are based more on who is working with the group and less on a sense of friendship; more on the present than on memory or loyalty to the past.

When "O'Brien" meets up with Jorgenson, he realizes how much anger has come to control him. He almost forgives him, but instead keeps alive the tension between them. More important than making peace, "O'Brien" acts out his need for making war, something that he desperately missed being stationed on a base. He needed an enemy more than a friend. He alienates Sanders by trying to hatch a plot against Jorgenson, but continues in his plan by signing on with Azar. Here we see "O'Brien" intentionally following a course that separates him more from his old "friends" because revenge and waging war on Jorgenson have become his most important purpose.

This new, personal warfare shows "O'Brien" how much the war has changed him from what he was to a machine of anger and revenge. He yearns for action, danger, and violence. He creates an enemy in order to wage war. He also recognizes that he is not fighting for an idea as large or potentially noble as "patriotic zeal," but solely for a personal vendetta.

So with much effort, "O'Brien" finds a way back into the war; his new enemy is Jorgenson. His ally, though, teaches him not only how far the war has changed him but also that he is not the weapon that he imagines. Azar takes the game too far, seeing "O'Brien" not as a soldier eager to engage the enemy but as a "disgusting...case" who feels more sympathy for Jorgenson. Azar's relentless assault on Jorgenson teaches "O'Brien" that his lust for revenge and combat, his covert, underhanded cruelty has made him not a soldier, but an enemy—he recoils not out of sympathy for Jorgenson but out of disgust in himself and what he has become. Even worse, he discovers that Azar joins with him not out of friendship, but out of a personal need for cruel humor. So "O'Brien" has lost his friends, his memories, his moral superiority, and all his anger; he is left "trembling...hugging himself, rocking" on the ground. This is the story of the complete defeat of a man. His reconciliation to Jorgenson is out of situation, not amnesty, but then again so were all of his relations.

Glossary

Gene Autry (1907–1998) Western movie star known as the "Singing Cowboy."

shipped off to Japan To be sent to an American military hospital in Japan, usually for serious wounds.

gangrene Decay of tissue in a part of the body when the blood supply is obstructed by injury or disease.

VC Viet Cong.

Highway 1 Major throughway for transportation through Vietnam.

Harmon Killebrew (b. 1936) a baseball player known as a power hitter who slugged home runs. He had a 22-year career with Washington, Minnesota, and Kansas City.

boonies   Boondocks; hinterland.

stand-down   A period of rest for combat soldiers during which they return to a base and halt all operations except security.

salt tabs   Tablets made of salt that servicemen placed along the inside of their cheeks to forestall dehydration by hastening the production of saliva.

a couple of klicks   Two kilometers.

Charlie Cong   Viet Cong.

Mary Hopkins   Folk singer from the mid-1960s whose hit single was "Those Were the Days" from the album *Postcards*.

trip flare   A flare rigged to ignite when an intruder moves a thin wire hidden along the outside perimeter of a base or encampment meant to signal the approach of enemy troops.

American Legion   An organization of veterans of the armed forces of the U.S., founded in 1919.

Night Life

Summary

Mitchell Sanders tells O'Brien a story about Rat Kiley: Due to rumors of North Vietnamese Army buildup in an area, Rat's platoon begins to move only at night and only off the main trails, struggling with the heavy foliage of the rain forest. They sleep in the day, which is difficult for Rat, who could feel tension and strain, causing him at first to become quiet and then to become nervous and jumpy. He starts talking about swarms of bugs and the strange strains of bugs in Vietnam. He scratches his bug bites, clawing them and finally scratching them until they become open sores. He eventually breaks down in front of Sanders, explaining that he is scared, but not normal scared. He sees pictures in his head of his fellow soldiers, but not their whole bodies, only parts and organs. He begins to see his own. Finally the tension gets to him and he shoots himself in the foot, a war wound that would rotate him out of the combat area. Lt. Cross says he would vouch that it was an accident, and Rat is flown to Japan to recover.

Commentary

Style & Language

O'Brien begins this vignette typically, at the end of the story. We know that Rat Kiley gets "hurt," but we do not know how badly and the nature of the wound. The story then moves almost nowhere as we know how it will end before it begins. Like so many of O'Brien's vignette, the point is not what happens as much as why it happens.

"Night Life" is about the precarious balance that a soldier keeps. In this case, what upsets the balance is a change in routine. It does not matter exactly what the routine is, just that something has changed. Despite the joke that they were all living the night life, the switch from days to nights made it a tense time for everyone. The tension simply overtakes Rat more than the others, but they all feel it. O'Brien shows us how unstable they all were, and by what a thin thread they were holding onto their control, whatever control they had.

Within the change is the element of night, itself a terrifying concept. O'Brien delivers a vivid account of the complete darkness of night in Vietnam and how it affects the company. The inability to blink or see any light for hours and hours, day after day, bears down on the troops, and for whatever reason (again, the element of randomness indicating that none of them were safer than any other), even more heavily on Rat Kiley.

Character Insight

Rat switches from intense silence to verbose babbling, searching desperately for a way to cope with this disruption to his routine and to regain control. Instead, he sinks further into himself, evident from his talk about body parts, poisons, and his compulsive scratching, externalizing much of the corporeal nature of his being a medic. He becomes focused on the decay and ruin of the human body. As the nights remain black, Rat sinks further and further down to the point of real fear. Rat was afraid of himself, a much more terrifying enemy than any in Vietnam. He was afraid of what he might do if he truly lost it.

Finally, he shoots himself in the foot. O'Brien makes it the climax of the story, so we might believe that Rat snapped all the way. Even though O'Brien could have sensibly said that the shooting came when Riley snapped, he does not say that specifically, even after phrases like "he lost his cool" and "Kiley finally hit a wall." Because he does not, it is just as plausible that Rat shoots himself to keep from going crazy. His injury not only concentrated on his body, a mark of his particular fixation, but also got him evacuated from the scene. O'Brien never tells for certain whether Rat's self-inflicted wound is a result of his fear or an attempt to master it.

Glossary

Nam   Shorthand for the Vietnam War, used by soldiers and veterans.

No Doz   Caffeine pills used to keep one awake.

defoliant   A chemical substance that causes leaves to fall from growing plants.

DDT   A powerful insecticide effective upon contact; its use is restricted by law due to damaging environmental effects.

snipe hunt   A futile search for something that does not exist.

The Lives of the Dead

Summary

O'Brien explains that stories can bring the dead back to life through the act of remembering. He describes the first dead body he saw in Vietnam, that of an old Vietnamese man. Others in the platoon spoke to the corpse in a mildly mocking way, but O'Brien could not even go near the body. The men proposed a toast to the dead man, but O'Brien would not join in. He tells Kiowa that the dead man reminded him of a girl he used to know.

O'Brien then segues into the story of a particular girl named Linda. Though O'Brien was only nine years old at the time, he believed he was in love with Linda, also age nine. He believed that their love was a mature love, not childish love. In spring of 1956, young O'Brien escorted Linda on their first date, chaperoned by O'Brien's parents. They went to a World War II movie whose premise was tricking the Germans by dumping the corpse of a soldier in a British officer's uniform and planting misleading documents on him. The premise upset O'Brien but he saw Linda smiling at the screen.

Linda began wearing the red cap she wore on their date to school, and her classmates teased her about it. O'Brien wishes that he would have stood up to her main instigator, Nick Veenhof, but he didn't. During class, Nick returned to his desk after sharpening his pencil and deliberately pulled off Linda's cap. Most of her hair was gone, and she wore a large bandage covering stitches across the back of her head. Linda suffered from a tumor in her brain, and she lived only through that summer. Nick told O'Brien that she had died, and O'Brien left school and went home. At home, he closed his eyes and tried to make her come back to life. In his mind, he saw her and she was healthy. She asked him why he was crying, and he answered that it was because she was dead. She told him to stop crying because it did not matter.

O'Brien then recalls how in Vietnam they had also had ways to make the dead seem alive again through the way they walked and thought about the dead. They kept the dead alive with stories, like the stories of Ted Lavender's death and those Rat Kiley told and embellished.

Returning to his memory of Linda, O'Brien describes how his father took him to the funeral home to view the body. O'Brien recalls how he made up stories so that Linda would appear in his dreams. They would talk and walk and ice skate in his dreams, and Linda would offer insights into life and death. At age 43, O'Brien still dreams Linda alive and he can see her in his dreams, as he can see Kiowa and Ted Lavender and others. Middle-aged O'Brien, a successful writer, realizes that he is trying to save his childhood self, Timmy, with a story.

Commentary

In this final chapter, the various threads of the work are finally woven together to form a cohesive message. Each of the major themes is illuminated as each of the major stories is retold. The cohesive core of the chapter is the present of "O'Brien" and his practice of what he referred to as his "Good Form" previously in the book: He objectifies his own experience, writing about himself alternating between the first- and third-person narrative voices.

"O'Brien" employs language and storytelling to postpone loss. This can be seen through the paradox of the chapter's title; "O'Brien" does bring characters back to life, imagining and animating them beyond the limits of tangible, sensory life. It is a kind of escapism, a way to think about a situation from another vantage point to understand it in a different way. Throughout the novel, characters employ this kind of mental escapism when thinking of home and other memories because it provides a familiar comfort and a way to impose meaning on events.

Literary
Device

The narrative situation that O'Brien presents in the final chapter is complicated because it tries to make sense of many of the stories that have been told and retold throughout. He offers readers a story within a story within a story. The general frame is one of an author and veteran thinking about Vietnam. As the author recollects and presents a story about animating the dead—the scene with the toast to the dead Vietnamese—another story within that story unfolds, O'Brien recollecting the death of his childhood friend, Linda. This layer of stories characterizes the power of stories as devices for ordering the events of life and figuring out one's response to those events.

O'Brien also revisits the problem of defining a "war story" as if it were a definitive genre. As the sequence of "O'Brien's" memories and O'Brien's stories unfold, the "war story" of the dead Vietnamese man gives way to become a story about love that demonstrates the power of stories to memorialize the dead. Symbolically, memorials are for the living more so than they are for the dead. They serve as reminders and as mediums for those who have lost someone or something to focus their grief on. Memorials exist at the intersection of the past and the present, and they also help the living remember that they are alive, which ultimately is the denouement of this chapter and the novel: The stories serve to save Timmy's life. And the impetus for the stories in the first place is the deep longing "Tim" and "Timmy" feel, like Lt. Cross' longing for Martha's love, like Rat's despondent slaughter of the baby buffalo, and how these become "O'Brien's" memorial to the men of Alpha Company, bridging the temporal gap between past and present and the epistemological gap between story and meaning.

Glossary

sniper   A soldier who shoots from a hidden position.

jeez   Euphemism for Jesus, used variously to express surprise, anger, annoyance and so on.

mind trip   Refers to a state of drug-altered reality.

The Man Who Never Was (c. 1956)   A movie which was a spy thriller about a World War II British spy trying to fool the Nazis into believing false plans for a British invasion of Greece. His nemesis is a German spy who tries to verify the identity of the British corpse on whom these false plans were planted.

CHARACTER ANALYSES

The following character analyses delve into the physical, emotional, and psychological traits of the literary work's major characters so that you might better understand what motivates these characters. The writer of this study guide provides this scholarship as an educational tool by which you may compare your own interpretations of the characters. Before reading the character analyses that follow, consider first writing your own short essays on the characters as an exercise by which you can test your understanding of the original literary work. Then, compare your essays to those that follow, noting discrepancies between the two. If your essays appear lacking, that might indicate that you need to re-read the original literary work or re-familiarize yourself with the major characters.

"Tim O'Brien" 88

Lt. Jimmy Cross 89

Norman Bowker 90

Mary Anne Bell 91

Kiowa 92

Rat Kiley 92

Linda 93

Henry Dobbins 94

"Tim O'Brien"

O'Brien is the most complex character in the novel, particularly so because we see him at three different stages of development. O'Brien the writer/narrator, "O'Brien" the soldier, and Timmy O'Brien the young boy all possess different thoughts and emotional understandings, each of which are in tension with the others. Part of O'Brien's goal as writer/narrator is to emphasize these tensions. For example, each of these characters grapples differently with the concept of death. Timmy learned at a young age to accept death; soldier "O'Brien" attempts to retrieve that lesson to deal with death in war; O'Brien the writer connects these two approaches, emphasizing the importance of memory to his ultimate understanding of death. This type of connection and understanding of death and loss comes out of the conflict O'Brien feels as he attempts to reconcile these different phases of his life. The conflict between the three different "O'Briens" manifests itself as pain and guilt, two qualities that paradoxically motivate O'Brien to seek wellness, and simultaneously creates for him a rich reservoir for his storytelling.

It is important to remember that O'Brien authors a personal war autobiography. He constantly reflects on and interrogates choices he has made, and invites his reader to do the same. For example, O'Brien derides himself as a coward and then directly addresses his readers, soliciting from them what they would do in his situation. The audience, then, becomes part of the novel; in other words, O'Brien pulls his readers into an intimate and highly personal dialogue with him. A close reader, however, will scrutinize O'Brien's believability and call into question his reliability as a narrator. O'Brien may not be the coward he claims, because he makes readers believe that they have a fuller and less-biased perspective of O'Brien than he does. The reader, for example, can weigh O'Brien's purported cowardice against his obligation to duty. O'Brien gives his readers a unique insight into "O'Brien" by more information about the interior feelings of "O'Brien" than are usually represented in a fictional work. The reader learns the history of the character, and therefore develops a sort of hindsight in interpreting "O'Brien's" actions.

The quality that best describes O'Brien is his capacity for introspection and reflective thought, leading directly to his use of memory in the novel. Of paramount importance to O'Brien the writer is his need to remember people and events from the past, to incorporate lessons learned (or not learned) into his present life. One way to understand how O'Brien becomes a writer is that writing is a way to manifest the past—writing is memory.

"O'Brien's" preoccupation with memory and re-memory derives in part from his inability to readjust to civilian life and forget his Vietnam experience. Though O'Brien attempts to make a case that his transition out of war was easy, he exhibits symptoms of post-traumatic stress disorder, including war-related depression, isolation, survival guilt, anxiety reactions, and nightmares. Writing is, in part, an attempt to quiet these things. Rather than forgetting his past, O'Brien confronts and reconfronts the various traumas of his life to resolve some of the elements of chaos he still feels thirty years later. He seeks not an end, but a resolution, and not through denial, but through memory.

A deeply affected and sensitive individual, the "O'Brien" character spends the novel searching for an emotional home, a feeling that he had as young boy in love and which he will never encounter again. O'Brien mourns the loss of innocence he felt growing up as a boy in the Midwest and feels a sense of betrayal from the community whose cherished, misguided, and uninformed beliefs sent him to war.

Lt. Jimmy Cross

Lt. Cross functions as a metaphor for the war, specifically its lack of meaningful structure. Like the war, Lt. Cross is characterized by a lack of definite purpose. Lt. Cross's role as leader of Alpha Company should be that of a strong leader who gives his troops clear instructions for gaining measurable advantage over the enemy. The nature of the Vietnam War, however, makes this kind of leadership impossible because the steps to achieve the objective of the war are undefined and obfuscated. Similar to battles and operations that constituted the war, Cross fails to demonstrate the clear ability to fulfill his role.

Lt. Cross is a weak leader because the traditional training he received is at stark odds with what he encounters in-country. His training forced him to be concerned more with marching in line, following preset maps, and keeping guns clean—following pre-decided standard operating procedures—rather than adapting to his environment and the attitude of his men. He was the leader of Alpha Company but never a true member of it, separating himself from his men in order to maintain a position of authority that he could never maintain if not for his superior rank. He never demonstrates leadership, but instead is granted it by decree. He lives for the knowledge that he is a leader, but is constantly afraid of that role. For example, Lt. Cross attempts to persuade himself of his own competence by relying on standard operating procedure after

Lavender is killed as a means to exonerate himself from feelings of personal culpability in Lavender's death as well as his pathetic neediness for Martha's love.

Cross's other character defect is his personal and emotional inability to lead Alpha Company. He jealously guards a photograph of Martha, a girl who is not his girlfriend, to maintain a strong link to love and his life at home. He fails to recognize, however, how love and war are connected, relying instead on his love for Martha as an escape from war. He cannot be both in love and in war; just as his relationship with Martha is a fiction, so is his ability to perform his soldierly duties. By loving, therefore, he actively resists his duty as a leader—he withdraws from leadership and Vietnam.

Cross is a foil to "O'Brien" because Timmy and Linda share a true love story and Cross and Martha do not. Martha is the object of Cross's sexual desire, Linda is not the subject of O'Brien's; Martha prevents Cross from being a soldier, Linda teaches Timmy about death. O'Brien's story is a true love story; Cross's is a war story; the primary function Cross serves in the novel is to demonstrate how sometimes stories are not cathartic, but sources of denial.

Norman Bowker

Bowker arrives in Vietnam operating within a schema of World War II soldiering. He believes, according to O'Brien, that what marks men as courageous are medals and service awards. Because of and in spite of this belief, Bowker has an active emotional life, an intensity of feeling about the atrocities he experienced in Vietnam, especially Kiowa's death. These feelings are not directed out toward the world as anger, but instead are turned in upon him, and they become self-loathing and extreme survivor guilt. O'Brien describes Bowker as someone who "did not know what to feel." Bowker himself could not find words to describe his feelings, and instead turns to O'Brien to tell his story for him.

Bowker connects "O'Brien" the soldier with O'Brien the writer. He operates as a figment of O'Brien's imagination, allowing him to move between the war and storytelling, providing a purpose and a story for O'Brien to tell. This stands in contrast to Bowker's actions in the novel, and points to what motivated him to take his own life: the lack of an objective.

Bowker embodies the paradox between the need for emotional truth and the pain many feel in expressing it. The Bowker character is most essential to the novel as fodder about which O'Brien creates a fictional story. He asks O'Brien to write his story, and when he reads it, asks him to revise it to reflect more of his feeling of intimate loss. Bowker teaches O'Brien how to articulate pain through storytelling, the particular pain of Kiowa's death to the wastefulness of war. Without this experience of articulating trauma through storytelling, O'Brien asserts that he too could have been trapped in the same emotional paralysis as Bowker. Bowker also helps O'Brien realize how writing helped him to avoid a similar fate.

Mary Anne Bell

Even more than the American soldiers in Vietnam, Mary Anne Bell represents the outsider, someone who does not belong where she is. Like Rat Kiley's disturbed response to conducting operations only during the night in "Night Life," the story of Mary Anne emphasizes what happens when someone's surroundings affect her. Mary Anne is also emblematic of transformation, specifically, the loss of innocence to experience. Similar to how the "green" medic Jorgenson is apt to make mistakes, Mary Anne is greener than any man in the novel. She arrives in Vietnam not only unprepared for war but also not intending to take part in it. Her transformation from a pretty girl wearing culottes to an animal-like hunter who wears a necklace of tongues parallels and exaggerates the change all young men went through in Vietnam, such as "O'Brien" who went from a boy who liked school to the man who plotted a sadistic revenge against Jorgenson.

O'Brien leaves out the conclusion to the tale about Mary Anne, instead letting her character pass into the realm of folklore. Rather than allowing us to know what becomes of someone (like himself) who undergoes a violent loss of innocence, we are left wondering how war affects a person, and to what ends of time that person will continue to feel its effect. The one piece of "knowledge" that Mary Anne's story teaches us is that once innocence is lost, it can never be regained. Unlike O'Brien or Bowker, however, when Mary Anne loses her innocence, she becomes an agent of primal instinct.

Finally, Mary Anne is the most real example of love in the novel. Although Lt. Cross and Henry Dobbins carry keepsakes that remind them of love, Mark Fossie is the only soldier who brings his girl to him.

Mary Anne's rapid descent from girlfriend and lover to warrior is the most blatant example in the novel of O'Brien linking love and war. Truth, to O'Brien, is an emotion, like Alpha Company believing in the story of Mary Anne when they knew they could not fully trust its storyteller, Rat Kiley. To O'Brien, love and war are not just connected; love and war are the same in that both refuse to let life interfere with emotion. Mary Anne is one of the "truest" characters in the novel because she lives off of her emotions and slips so easily between a posture of love and one of war.

Kiowa

Kiowa is the emotional compass of Alpha Company, the one who gets everyone else to talk. Kiowa tries to comfort "O'Brien" after he kills the North Vietnamese soldier, and it is to Kiowa that Dobbins opens up about his respect for the clergy. The night before Kiowa is killed, the young soldier is in a tent speaking to him about his girlfriend left behind.

Kiowa helps "O'Brien" by easing his transitions. He makes "O'Brien" more comfortable when he arrives at the war, talking to him about the others' jokes about corpses, and he tries to get "O'Brien" to talk about the Vietnamese soldier he killed. "O'Brien" tells the story of Linda to Kiowa. It is from Kiowa, therefore, that "O'Brien" learns the importance of communicating, leading eventually to his becoming a writer. In some ways, Kiowa's death is what makes "O'Brien" a writer, a teller of stories. When he returns to Vietnam with Katherine, he takes her to the site of Kiowa's death in the field. Although "O'Brien" does not tell her the story of Kiowa, he brings her to that site so that he might pass the story on, just as he will pass on the story of how he killed a man when he feels Katherine is ready to hear it.

Rat Kiley

Rat Kiley is the prototypical storyteller, always relating something that happened somewhere else. He teaches "O'Brien" the power of the story. Even an unreliable storyteller, as Rat is, can still command the attention and belief of his audience because people like hearing his stories. Rat is well regarded, even though people knew him to exaggerate. He is integral to the life of Alpha Company—the medic who helps the others out. When O'Brien was shot the first time, Rat helped him, saved him. He is a combination of teller and doer, the man who could tell a story as well as patch a wound.

Rat also teaches us the limits of what a man can take. Rat shoots himself in the foot as a result of the company switching to a routine of night-movement for two weeks. As night is a common metaphor for death, we understand how Rat deals with the new, pressing presence of death around him. Rat's paranoia, his visions of body parts, is his fear manifesting itself, and because he is such an enthralling storyteller, he makes the others in the company (as well as the readers) feel his fear too. Where Bowker commits suicide and Mary Anne Bell becomes an agent of the wild, Kiley decides to remove himself from death by shooting himself in the foot. All of these characters demonstrate how each person deals differently with the limits of innocence and human understanding when confronted by something as powerful and terrifying as war.

Linda

Linda is an important symbol in the novel, representing the function of memory, love, and death. Timmy's fourth-grade sweetheart, Linda provides O'Brien with the idea of true love, a love as innocent as his Midwestern upbringing. On their date, they see a war movie, establishing a first connection between love and war. Added to this is the fact that O'Brien's story about Linda turns into the story of her death. The story of Linda sets up one of O'Brien's primary themes in the novel: the inextricable link between love and death. It is not that Timmy loves Linda and then she dies, rather that he loves her because she dies—love and death are the same. It is his love for Linda that allows an older "O'Brien" to go to war, and later to write about it. The whole novel, then, is about love and death, about Timmy and Linda.

Like Bowker, Linda gives O'Brien a reason to write. In his vision of her after her death, Linda tells O'Brien to "stop crying," that death "doesn't matter." Indeed, O'Brien uses writing to tell the story of Linda, to give her life again, or as he puts it, to "save Linda's life." Writing is creative; it counters the destruction of death and war. Bowker's need to have O'Brien tell his story is the same as O'Brien's need to remember Linda through writing, which is itself an act that sustains life by animating the dead.

Henry Dobbins

Henry Dobbins' actions are driven by his sincerity, respectfulness, kindness, and faith. Dobbins is not a complex character; he exhibits a resounding genuineness in his actions, such as reprimanding Azar as he mimicked the dancing of a traumatized Vietnamese girl. Similarly, Dobbins' character and personality are revealed as he expresses his thoughts about joining the clergy when he and Kiowa discuss religion in "Church." Although he cannot understand the monks' language, he shows them kindness, respecting the sanctity of their church and speaking to them in what little Vietnamese he knows. O'Brien makes Dobbins a different model for a soldier than Azar, who is particularly savage and immature, and the others in Alpha Company: He is a great soldier, but he is neither bloodthirsty nor obnoxious. Dobbins represents the good intentions of middle America.

Another notable attribute of Dobbins is his intense commitment to following his moral code. Just as Dobbins is "drawn toward sentimentality" in his personal beliefs and his approach to the war, he is similarly insulated from the psychological and physical trauma of war through the power of his belief. Dobbins focuses this power on, and believes that his faith stems from, a pair of pantyhose that are his personal talisman. He believes himself safe from harm as long as he keeps the pantyhose, and he is. For example, Dobbins trips a land mine—an event that usually kills—without the mine detonating. Dobbins attributes this miracle to his faith in the pantyhose, and through this event, he "turned [Alpha Company] into a platoon of believers." Dobbins demonstrates to us that what you believe in is not as important as simply believing in something, and he teaches his fellow soldiers to believe in his story of defying death.

CRITICAL ESSAYS

On the pages that follow, the writer of this study guide provides critical scholarship on various aspects of O'Brien's *The Things They Carried*. These interpretive essays are intended solely to enhance your understanding of the original literary work; they are supplemental materials and are not to replace your reading of *The Things They Carried*. When you're finished reading *The Things They Carried*, and prior to your reading this study guide's critical essays, consider making a bulleted list of what you think are the most important themes and symbols. Write a short paragraph under each bullet explaining why you think that theme or symbol is important; include at least one short quote from the original literary work that supports your contention. Then, test your list and reasons against those found in the following essays. Do you include themes and symbols that the study guide author doesn't? If so, this self test might indicate that you are well on your way to understanding original literary work. But if not, perhaps you will need to re-read *The Things They Carried*.

The Things They Carried in a Historical Context 96

Narrative Structure in The Things They Carried 97

Style and Storytelling in The Things They Carried 98

The Things They Carried and Loss of Innocence 99

The Things They Carried and Questions of Genre 101

The Things They Carried in a Historical Context

Though Vietnam has a long history of conflict over its independence from its founding in 208 B.C., U.S. involvement in the affairs of Vietnam began to crystallize during the final years of World War II. At the Potsdam Conference, the Allied powers determined that Britain would occupy Vietnam and force out Japanese troops occupying the area south of the sixteenth parallel. After a summer of internal political unrest in Vietnam, in September 1945, British forces arrived. Though Vietnam had long been a French colonial interest, the Vietnamese resisted French influence and clamored for independence, even attempting to enlist the United States' assistance. In early 1946, the French did assent to recognizing limited Vietnamese independence and Ho Chi Minh as the leader of the Democratic Republic of Vietnam. During that year, the Vietminh attacked French military forces and provoked the French into war, in which the United States supported their French allies throughout the Truman presidency. The French began to reassert their power over Vietnam, but the Chinese and Soviet governments allied themselves with Ho Chi Minh.

Bao Dai, the leader of the French-recognized faction, also claimed that his party, and not Minh's, had authority over the country. By 1950, the Truman administration had begun sending American military advisors to Vietnam to support the French. Eventually, the United States began lending financial support to France's war against Minh supporters. While western nations were outlining such policies as those set forth by the Geneva Convention (1954) and SEATO (1954), internal division within Vietnam continued to escalate. Fearing the threat of the expanse of Communism throughout the Pacific Asian area, the United States, during the Eisenhower and Kennedy administrations, continued aiding the French, until the number of U.S. military personnel deployed to Southeast Asia numbered nearly 20,000. Under the Johnson administration, the U.S. destroyers *Maddox* and *C. Turner Joy* received fire from North Vietnamese boats, and President Johnson reacted by ordering an aerial assault of North Vietnam. Only a few days after this incident, Congress passed the Gulf of Tonkin Resolution, which extended to the president the necessary authority to conduct war, though war was never officially declared.

Within months, the first combat-ready unit was deployed to U.S. Marines headquarters at Da Nang in March, 1965. U.S. involvement continued to steadily increase, and by the close of 1967 over a million American troops were in Vietnam, despite the growing sentiment of the American public to stop or withdraw from the war. The undeclared "war" eventually became the United States' longest foreign policy engagement. After years of intense battle, the United States withdrew the last combat troops from Vietnam in March 1973. More than 1.2 million Americans served in the war; nearly 60,000 died in service.

The objective that the United States supported—in short, preventing Vietnam from becoming a communist foothold—was never realized. In April 1975, Saigon surrendered to the communist revolutionaries; the following year, the Socialist Republic of Vietnam was declared.

Narrative Structure in *The Things They Carried*

The Things They Carried is not easily characterized as a novel or autobiography or short story collection. The book is comprised of 22 short pieces that are referential to one another. Though individual pieces can stand alone, and some were published singly or anthologized, the distinct pieces are meant to comprise a whole meditative novel.

One narrative technique that O'Brien uses is repetition. O'Brien frequently retells certain incidents, often adding incremental detail with each telling. One example of this is the scene of Kiowa's death, which, retold five times, is the core of most of the novel's action and the catalyst for most characters' development. Students often overlook the importance of this repetition by mistaking it as redundancy. Instead, the repetition is a stylistic technique O'Brien employs to illuminate the truth of a story by adding and subtracting telling detail. The effect of this for an astute reader is a feeling that simulates "O'Brien's" intense obsession with the stories he tells and retells because they run through his memory almost constantly.

O'Brien's novel is untraditional in a second narrative sense as well, due in part to the non-linear presentation of the novel's action. O'Brien does not maintain temporal continuity; he jumps from the past to the present and then to the distant past and then back to the present. In a way, this constant memory shifting leads the reader down a path of memory similar to O'Brien's. In other words, O'Brien forces an experience of recollections leading to other memories and new insights on his reader, creating an emotional response to the novel in the reader. This path of memory—which is congruent to O'Brien's own—more actively involves the reader in a constant dialogic interplay with the novel. For readers, as for O'Brien, certain events and details recall the details and events of other stories. By using a narrative technique that constantly generates new contexts in which to revisit stories, such as that when O'Brien recalls Linda when contemplating a dead body he sees in Vietnam, he creates new meanings through shifting juxtapositions.

Style and Storytelling in *The Things They Carried*

Tim O'Brien crafts an artfully unique story in *The Things They Carried,* from the scraps of an experience of war that is not particularly more extraordinary or different than others who served in Vietnam through innovative application of style. Style is *how* an author tells a story, and O'Brien demonstrates his style twice in the novel: He presents a certain style as the author Tim O'Brien, and he presents another as his fictional characterization, also named "Tim O'Brien." This decisive and ingenious creation brings about an interesting tension between what is true and what is not quite true and produces both a meditative tone and a sense of distrust in the author that runs throughout the novel like a hairline crack in a foundation.

This, too, gives rise to the meta-textuality of the novel. O'Brien's style is one marked by examining an event from a distance, either spatially or temporally, and the creation of "O'Brien" allows for this distance. O'Brien comments on the usefulness of telling stories by creating a character who shares his name and vocation; he demonstrates in fiction what he does in real life, writing stories about the past to better understand it.

Meta-textuality refers to art that comments on its own process or purpose, and the "O'Brien" character practices this as well. Through the vignette "Notes" especially, O'Brien/"O'Brien" comments on the process of writing. The rationale behind "Speaking of Courage" is described in great detail. The effect of this supposedly honest and deliberate style of telling readers more than just the story of Norman Bowker is double-edged. The chapter is both an honest exposition of how "Speaking of Courage" is a bastardized account of what happened the night Kiowa died, and a reminder that the author/narrator is stylistically slippery and not fully reliable.

O'Brien frequently challenges readers to believe or disbelieve aspects of his stories and blurs the boundaries between fiction and truth. By calling the veracity of stories into question, O'Brien underscores the overall style that defines *The Things They Carried:* constantly changing at random, unexpected, marked by telling juxtapositions, diffuse, not easily defined. The combination of these stylistic approaches, paired with the questioning of a story's veracity, evokes deliberately a sense of uneasiness in the reader. Style, for O'Brien, is an overarching theme of the novel, because these appellations of randomness, unevenness, and lack of definition can be applied to the Vietnam War, which also becomes a meta-textual comment on how stories—in this case the actual Vietnam War—are received and perceived.

The Things They Carried and Loss of Innocence

One of the main themes of the novel is the allure of war. This trope, common in war literature, is made more complex here as O'Brien adds the layers of a Conrad-esque "heart of darkness" fascination in the character of Mary Anne.

The seductive allure of war is inextricably linked to the tendencies of human nature in O'Brien's novel. War, more specifically the act of killing, acts as a catalyst for some individuals, causing them to become primal versions of themselves, to become less human, to become killing machines. O'Brien revisits this idea numerous times throughout the text, adding subtle variations on the theme as he introduces different characters that struggle with the same core issue. O'Brien initially creates this tension by offering the counterpoint of O'Brien's daily work duty of declotting slaughtered pigs with his anxiety about his imminent service as a soldier in Vietnam. O'Brien merges the ideas of killing with animals, a symbolic linkage he revisits by describing the soldiers of Alpha Company as animal-like, "humping" their packs and "saddling up" their gear.

O'Brien struggles to hold onto the obverse of this animalism, this barbarism, which is a sort of hyper-civility. He succeeds in doing this by continually offering a highly self-conscious and self-aware cultural criticism that frequently draws on the archetypal works that are the foundation of western civilization like Plato's *Republic*.

Contrary to the protagonist "O'Brien's" experiential insulation from Vietnamese culture, which is a kind of "uncivilized other" according to the terms of U.S. rhetoric that largely defined the war, Mary Anne Bell is a character who deliberately strove for cultural immersion. For "O'Brien," the landscape and the Vietnamese occupying that landscape, such as the elderly Vietnamese men who watch him revisit the spot where Kiowa perished, are mostly incidental. Mary Anne actively sought out the ways of the Vietnamese, not just to observe from a distance, but to participate in if possible. Mary Anne, who should have behaved according to accepted Western norms, becomes so much a part of the landscape of Vietnam that she becomes "unnatural" to Mark and Rat. For example, the humming they hear coming from the Greenies' hut is freaky and unnatural, somehow not human, but it is Mary Anne's humming. And particularly as a female, she should be "domesticated" and behave in accordance with the readers' expectations of a young woman in a decade prior to the women's liberation movement. Instead she is seduced by the foreign landscape of Vietnam—one which "O'Brien" resists and barely describes—and is reduced to her animal-like primal self, a killing machine. Finally, opposite to "O'Brien," Mary Anne shows no resistance to the landscape, and has the agility and prowess to slip into the jungle like an adept, predatory jungle animal ready for the hunt.

O'Brien relies on symbolism Joseph Conrad created in *Heart of Darkness* to connect the landscape of Vietnam to the landscape of immorality that Mary Anne succumbs to and "O'Brien" resists. Mary Anne becomes a part of what O'Brien/"O'Brien" most vehemently opposes and what O'Brien/"O'Brien" most fears: the struggle between the light and dark forces of human nature and the predominance of the darker forces. Just as the character of Mary Anne echoes Conrad's character, Kurtz, "O'Brien" is a cousin to Conrad's character, Marlow. Like Marlow, O'Brien struggles against his imagination and the fantastic cultural stories that feed it, in "O'Brien's" case, the stories of World War II he learned from movies and stories of his father's generation. Ultimately, O'Brien shields himself from a fate similar to Mary Anne's through the way he employs stories, just as he did during the summer when he worked at the meatpacking plant, by forcing him to look at the struggle between dark and light within himself.

The Things They Carried and Questions of Genre

Literary critic David Wyatt argues that "war refers, remembers, revises . . . war compulsively *alludes*."

This reminder is valuable in assigning O'Brien's novel to various genres. A genre is an established literary form that is characterized by a set of like qualities. *The Things They Carried* has membership in a number of genres, but is most commonly classified as a "war novel." As a genre, the war novel has a certain set of attributes that readers expect. O'Brien works within a long tradition of war literature, and, as Wyatt rightly suggests, *The Things They Carried* refers to works by O'Brien's predecessors. Clearly, O'Brien's novel recalls—in content form, and style—the work of those who defined modern war literature, namely Wilfred Owen, Stephen Crane, George Orwell, and Ernest Hemingway. While *The Things They Carried* most openly invokes Conrad's *Heart of Darkness,* a seminal text in the war novel genre that erects the dichotomy between innocence and experience (which also pervades *The Things They Carried*), the novel shares more generic qualities with the works of the other authors mentioned above.

For each of these writers, O'Brien included, war is chaotic, and writing about war, using words to understand an experience, is a way to impose order and control over that chaos. For each, the war is depicted at points with visceral and emotional intensity and overwhelming sensation. These authors yoke the glamour of war that this intensity can breed by creating a symbolic counterpoint to the war by means of a romantic subplot. Owen and Hemingway, for example, emphasize how the war experience, and the emotional and physical wounds of that experience, make men less desirable to women and alienate the broken, de-masculinized soldier from his world. Much of O'Brien's body of work resonates with this recurring theme.

Another characteristic of the modern war novel genre is the protagonist's constant propensity to make witness, to offer detailed accounts of minutiae, again as a coping mechanism to gain control over the chaos of war and to offer more than a story of loss by creating a story of survival. On a basic level, O'Brien's novel converses with and butts up against these generic themes.

Within the larger genre of war narratives is the Vietnam War genre. Copious amounts of Vietnam War-related fiction, non-fiction, and film proliferated after the war and in the mid-1980s, and events such as the creation of the Vietnam War Memorial helped to create public interest in talking about the Vietnam War. While this sub-genre refers to the more generic war literature genre, it possesses more particular attributes, deriving from the nature of the Vietnam War, that set it apart, such as wastefulness and failure.

The emergence of the Vietnam War genre coincided with a historical moment that gave rise to its searching reflexivity—as the first wave of post-Vietnam War literature and films were written and released, national morale was at a low. The nation that had struggled with the Vietnam War had also faced the Watergate scandal and now an economic downturn. The government was scrutinized and its infallibility continually interrogated by the public. Perhaps a parallel effect can be seen as writers, many of who were combatants, attempted to voice their feelings of love, anger, and disenchantment.

The standout works that followed the war share an acute sense of reflexivity, a sharp bent towards the subjective voice, and a vested interest in telling stories. While the predecessors of such works as Al Santoli's *Everything We Had,* Michael Herr's *Dispatches,* and Neil Sheeham's *A Bright, Shining Lie* surely are Owen, Crane, Hemingway, and specifically Orwell, the Vietnam War works are postmodern. In this sense, the Vietnam War genre is postmodern because of a hyper-self-awareness of form within literary form. O'Brien, Herr, and Santoli are obsessed by storytelling, and their writing is frequently about writing and the generation of stories themselves.

A sense of postmodernism is created through the interaction of three main similarities present in the Vietnam War literary genre. First, clearly delineated definitions of fiction and non-fiction are abandoned. In *The Things They Carried,* O'Brien fuses these modes of discourse. Second, verisimilitude becomes secondary to the interplay of form and style. Third, a highly self-aware, subjective (anti-)hero is the protagonist. *The Things They Carried* is, then, by definition a postmodern Vietnam War narrative. Because of its postmodern the Vietnam War genrequalities, it is at once a collection of stories and a novel, a piece of fiction and an autobiography (non-fiction), and war narrative and a Vietnam War narrative.

CliffsNotes Review

Use this CliffsNotes Review to test your understanding of the original text and reinforce what you've learned in this book. After you work through the review and essay questions, identify the quote section, and the fun and useful practice projects, you're well on your way to understanding a comprehensive and meaningful interpretation of Tim O'Brien's *The Things They Carried*.

Fill in the Blank

1. A former Alpha Company soldier, _____ committed suicide by hanging himself.

2. Reunited with "O'Brien" after the war, _____ was still preoccupied with his unrequited love for Martha.

3. _____, a soldier stationed near Tra Bong, had not anticipated the effects of the Vietnam experience on his girlfriend.

4. This character, _____, is the first whom "O'Brien" could see in his dreams.

5. This soldier, _____, was "O'Brien's" confidante, especially after "O'Brien" killed the unnamed Vietnamese soldier.

6. As a medic, this soldier experienced a failure of courage and nerve, but _____ later made amends with "O'Brien."

7. As a talisman, _____ carried his girlfriend's pantyhose around his neck.

8. This character, _____, gives "O'Brien" an "emergency fund."

9. An Alpha Company medic, _____ could not stand the strain of war and began to hallucinate.

10. This soldier, _____, stole a jackknife from Dave Jensen, one of his fellow soldiers.

11. While horseplaying with Rat Kiley, _____ was killed by accident.

12. This character, _____, believes that "O'Brien" should forget the war and write about something else

13. To get revenge on Bobby Jorgenson, "O'Brien" consorted with _____.

14. A former Alpha Company soldier, _____, returns to Vietnam and brings Kiowa's moccasins with him.

15. Because of a pact the two soldiers had made, _____ was relieved when he learned that Lee Strunk died from his battle wounds.

Answers: (1) Norman Bowker. (2) Jimmy Cross. (3) Mark Fossie. (4) Linda. (5) Kiowa. (6) Bobby Jorgenson. (7) Henry Dobbins. (8) Elroy Berdahl. (9) Rat Kiley. (10) Lee Strunk. (11) Curt Lemon. (12) Kathleen. (13) Azar. (14) "O'Brien." (15) Dave Jensen.

Identify the Quote: Find Each Quote in *The Things They Carried*

Read the following passages and identify the speaker, the person to whom the comment is directed, and the context of the quote.

1. "'I know it sounds far-out,' he'd tell us, 'but it's not like impossible or anything. We all heard plenty of wackier stories. Some guy comes back from the bush, tells you he saw the Virgin Mary out there, she was riding a goddamn goose or something. Everybody buys it. Everybody smiles and asks how fast she was going, did she have spurs on. Well, it's not like that. This Mary Anne wasn't no virgin but at least she was real. I saw it. When she came in through the wire that night, I was right there, I saw those eyes of hers, I saw how she wasn't even the same person no more.'"

2. "Forty-three years old, and the war occurred half a lifetime ago, and yet the remembering makes it now. And sometimes remembering will lead to a story, which makes it forever. That's what stories are for. Stories are for joining the past to future. Stories are for those late hours in the night when you can't remember how you got from where you were to where you are. Stories are for eternity, when memory is erased, when there is nothing to remember except the story."

3. "The day was cloudy. I passed through towns with familiar names, through the pine forests and down to the prairie, and then to Vietnam, where I was a soldier, and then home again. I survived, but it's not a happy ending. I was a coward. I went to the war."

4. "In any war story, but especially a true one, it's difficult to separate what happened from what seemed to happen. What seems to happen becomes its own happening and has to be told that way. The angles of vision are skewed. When a booby trap explodes, you close your eyes and duck and float outside yourself. When a guy dies, like Curt Lemon, you look away and then look back for a moment and then look away again. The pictures get jumbled; you tend to miss a lot. And then afterward, when you go to tell about it, there is always a surreal seemingness, which makes the story seem untrue, but which, in fact represents the hard and exact truth as it seemed."

5. "'The thing is,' he wrote, 'there's no place to go. Not just in this lousy little town. In general. My life, I mean. It's almost like I got killed over in Nam...Hard to describe. That night when Kiowa got wasted, I sort of sank down into the sewage with him. . . Feels like I'm still in deep shit.'"

6. "I'm not dead. But when I am, it's like. . . I don't know, I guess it's like being inside a book that nobody's reading...An old one. It's up on a library shelf, so you're safe and everything, but the book hasn't been checked out for a long, long time. All you can do is wait. Just hope somebody'll pick it up and start reading."

Answers: (1) Rat Kiley delivers this plea about the believability of the story about Mary Anne Bell that he tells to the men of Alpha Company. The quote is from the vignette, "Sweetheart of the Song Tra Bong," and refers to the seeming fanciful and unbelievable premise of the story of a young woman who becomes fascinated by the war. (2) The character "Tim O'Brien" addresses this passage to the reader at the close of the vignette, "Spin." The passage is part of the novel that is acts as writer's memoir, in this case, fictional character Tim O'Brien's memoir, wherein a writer reflects on how and why he thinks of and tells stories. This particular passage is characteristic of the novel's meta-textual qualities. (3) Again, character "Tim O'Brien" offers these lines in the final paragraph of "On the Rainy River," reflecting on his near fleeing to Canada. The lines are, of course, ironic and invite the reader of the fictional character's war autobiography to question his or her notions of what cowardice is. (4) Fictional character "O'Brien" offers these lines to clarify both how he remembers and how his memories are stitched into the quilt of a story. The scenes may be disjunctive, and when he recalls the details of the many horrific scenes he witnessed in Vietnam, the stories seem untrue, even to O'Brien. Yet, this quality that makes stories seem unbelievable is exactly what makes them so completely true—in other words, the actual scenes of war challenge what we think we know about war. The difference between our untested preconceived notions and the actual uncanny horrors of war is this sense of surrealism—that what seems impossible actually is true because it exceeds our notions of what we might have expected to see, feel, or encounter in war. (5) Norman Bowker writes these lines in a letter to "Tim O'Brien" in the vignette, "Speaking of Courage." Bowker describes how he was personally affected by Kiowa's death. More importantly, the subtextual meaning of the quote underlines the importance and absolute need to tell stories as a means for unburdening one's self from the emotional pressure that participating in a war and losing a friend in battle can create. (6) Linda .addresses "Timmy"—the boyhood incarnation of character "Tim O'Brien"—as an apparition in his dreams. This quote is the crux of the novel and offers the author's philosophy on death and the power of storytelling to animate the dead and bring them into the present as a way to bring one's self comfort.

Essay Questions

1. Given traditions of war literature, why does O'Brien write a war story that has no heroes? How do you think O'Brien defines "heroism"?

2. What is the place of women in a war story? Why does O'Brien need characters like Mary Anne, Kathleen, and Martha in his novel? What is the connection between love and war, if there is one?

3. How are "Tim O'Brien" the soldier and "Tim O'Brien" the writer different? How does the experience of one illuminate the experience of the other? How are these depictions of "O'Brien" in various stages of his life related to "Timmy"? What does "O'Brien" mean when he writes that he realizes writing "is as Tim trying to save Timmy's life with a story"?

4. Comment on three characters' loss of innocence in the novel, more specifically how these characters move from innocence of war to experience of the ravages of Vietnam. What is the catalyst for their change? Do you think these characters completely lose their innocence, and if they do, how does O'Brien demonstrate this?

5. Discuss three examples of O'Brien writing about writing or storytelling. How does this relate to O'Brien's decision to write his work as a series of vignettes or interrelated stories rather than as a traditional linear narrative?

6. What is the function of memory in the novel? According to O'Brien, does remembering the past preclude "endings" such as the ending of O'Brien's personal and emotional conflict over participation in the Vietnam War? Both Kathleen and Linda discuss "endings." With whose version do you think "O'Brien" ultimately agrees and why?

Practice Projects

1. Read the essay entitled "The Vietnam in Me" (*New York Times* Magazine [2 October 1994]: 48–57) that O'Brien wrote about his first return trip to Vietnam after his service ended. The fictionalized account of O'Brien's return to Vietnam differs sharply from the actual version that O'Brien glosses in his essay. The most significant difference is O'Brien's traveling companion. O'Brien does not have a daughter, as he creates in the character of Kathleen in the novel. Instead, he is accompanied by his then-girlfriend, a woman a number of years his junior. Compare the essays and think about the following questions. What does this difference tell us about O'Brien's philosophy of truth in storytelling? How does the essay illuminate your reading of the novel? How does it speak to the urgency of passing stories from one generation to another?

2. Research the anti-Vietnam War movement. What objections did the protestors have to the war? Find out what arguments they used against maintaining the war. What kind of rhetoric did they use? Research Vietnam veterans' involvement in the anti-war movement. Compare their arguments to O'Brien's objections to the war. Read other Vietnam veterans' war narratives, such as Ron Kovics' *Born on the Fourth of July* and Robert Mason's *Chickenhawk*, and compare their impressions of the war with the fictional "O'Brien's."

3. Simulate the original literary form that O'Brien invented for *The Things They Carried*. Write a fictionalized version of an event similar to one you have experienced. Create a fictional protagonist who shares your name and write a narrative and descriptive passage about what "you" see and think and do. After doing this, write a passage about *how* you wrote the paragraph and *why* you wrote it, simulating O'Brien's meta-fictive style.

4. Compare O'Brien's novel (or *The Soldier's Sweetheart*, a film based on the vignette, "Sweetheart of the Song Tra Bong") to films about the Vietnam War, such as Francis Ford Coppola's *Apocalypse Now* and Stanley Kubrick's *Full Metal Jacket*. Do the novel and the films share similar qualities? What are these qualities? How do you think they differ from those of the classic combat film genre that depict World War II and the Korean War. Research the film references O'Brien makes in the novel: John Wayne, *The Green Berets*, Audie Murphy, *The Man Who Never Was*. How do these examples he offers speak to this difference? How is he critiquing these references, and to what effect?

CliffsNotes Resource Center

The learning doesn't need to stop here. CliffsNotes Resource Center shows you the best of the best—links to the best information in print and online about Tim O'Brien and works written by and about him. And don't think that this is all we've prepared for you; we've put all kinds of pertinent information at www.cliffsnotes.com. Look for all the terrific resources at your favorite bookstore or local library and on the Internet. When you're online, make your first stop www.cliffsnotes.com, where you'll find more useful information about *The Things They Carried*.

Books

If you're looking for more information about Tim O'Brien and his other works, check out these publications.

Primary Sources

Northern Lights. New York: Delacorte/Seymour Lawrence, 1975.

If I Die in a Combat Zone, Box Me Up and Ship Me Home. 1973. Reprint, New York: Dell, 1983.

Going After Cacciato. 1978. Reprint, New York: Dell, 1989.

The Things They Carried. 1990. Reprint, New York: Penguin, 1991.

The Nuclear Age. 1985. Reprint, New York: Dell, 1993.

In the Lake of the Woods. 1994, Reprint, New York: Penguin, 1995.

"The Vietnam in Me." *New York Times Magazine* (2 October 1994): 48–57.

Secondary Sources

Baritz, Loren. *Backfire: A History of How American Culture Led Us into Vietnam and Made Us Fight the Way We Did*. New York: Morrow, 1985. Loren Baritz examines the national mindset that allowed America to be led into the long history of colonialism and civil war in Vietnam. By identifying and deconstructing the various myths that led America into war such as jingoistic idealism and the assertion of technological superiority, Baritz explains how a well-equipped superpower did not win a decisive victory over a mostly rural and war-torn nation.

Beidler, Philip D. *American Literature and the Experience of Vietnam*. Athens, Ga.: University of Georgia Press, 1982. Professor Beidler begins to define a Vietnam War literary genre by identifying and discussing characteristics common to fiction and non-fiction works that emerged out of the Vietnam War.

Gilbert, Marc Jason, ed. *The Vietnam War: Teaching Approaches and Resources*. New York: Greenwood, 1991. This informative book is an excellent resource for educators and for students who are looking for innovative ways to illuminate and understand the Vietnam War. Gilbert offers strategies for teaching Vietnam War literature and film as a means for getting at such war related issues as the history of Vietnam and the difficulty of readjustment after the war.

Herzog, Tobey C. *Tim O'Brien*. New York: Twayne Publishers, 1997. Herzog presents a detailed analysis of O'Brien's major works by identifying the major themes of his novels. This resource is particularly rich because many of the ideas Herzog explores are based on his interviews with O'Brien.

Kaplan, Steven. *Understanding Tim O'Brien*. Columbia, S.C.: University of South Carolina Press, 1995. Kaplan offers a comprehensive study of O'Brien, beginning first with a brief biography of the author that becomes essential for understanding much of O'Brien's works. Kaplan glosses O'Brien's major works in more than adequate detail, and explains how O'Brien's works fit in a wider context of war literature. His analysis and criticism of *The Things They Carried* is outstanding because of its understandability.

Karnow, Stanley. *Vietnam: A History*. New York: Viking, 1983. Considered to be the definitive history of the Vietnam War, Karnow's far-reaching account is based on the author's exhaustive work with primary documents and interviews with a wide variety of those who participated in the war, from the highest-ranking diplomats and commanders to front-line soldiers.

Wyatt, David. *Out of the Sixties: Storytelling and the Vietnam Generation*. Cambridge: Cambridge University Press, 1993. Wyatt's work is useful as a way for readers of O'Brien's books to understand the Vietnam era from a post-war perspective. Wyatt's thoughtful account of the need for storytelling complements O'Brien's meta-fictive narration.

Articles

Bates, Milton J. "Tim O'Brien's Myth of Courage." *Modern Fiction Studies* 33 (Summer 1987): 263–279.

Bohn, Maria S. "Can Stories Save Us? Tim O'Brien and the Efficacy of the Text." *Critique* 36 (Fall 1994): 2–15.

Calloway, Catherine. "Tim O'Brien: A Checklist." *Bulletin of Bibliography* 48 (March 1991): 6–11.

——————. " 'How to Tell a True War Story': Metafiction in *The Things They Carried.*" *Critique* 36 (Summer 1995): 249–257.

Horner, Carl S. "Challenging the Law of Courage and Heroic Identification in Tim O'Brien's *If I Die in a Combat Zone* and *The Things They Carried.*" *War, Literature, and the Arts: An International Journal of the Humanities* 11 (Spring-Summer 1999): 256–267.

Kaplan, Steven. "The Undying Uncertainty of the Narrator in Tim O'Brien's *The Things They Carried.*" *Critique* 35. (Fall 1993): 43–52.

Smith. Lorrie. " 'The Things Men Do': Gendered Subtext in Tim O'Brien's *Esquire* Stories." *Critique* 36 (Fall 1994): 16–39.

Volkmer, John. "Telling the 'Truth' about Vietnam: Episteme and Narrative Structure in *The Green Berets* and *The Things They Carried.*" *War, Literature, and the Arts: An International Journal of the Humanities* 11 (Spring-Summer 1999): 240–255.

Film

A Soldier's Sweetheart. Dir. Thomas Michael Donnelly. Perf. Kiefer Sutherland, Skeet Ulrich, and Georgina Cates. Paramount, 1998.

In the Lake of the Woods. Dir. Carl Schenkel. Independently produced/made for television, 1996.

Internet Resources

The Tim O'Brien Web page, www.illyria.com/tobhp.html—Enthusiastic fan site devoted to the literary works and career of Tim O'Brien. The site offers helpful links to reviews of O'Brien's work and articles and interviews about O'Brien's career. The site's highlight is an extensive guest book that readers use to exchange insights about O'Brien's work. The site also keeps a fairly up-to-date listing of O'Brien's public appearances.

PBS's POV: Stories After the War Home Page, www.pbs.org/pov/stories/index.html—This site was created in conjunction with the PBS documentary series *POV* to create a look at the Vietnam War through examining others' stories. The site is largely a forum for users to share their experiences and recollections of the war. The philosophy that underpins the site is that examining the impact of the war is key to understanding America today. Reader s of O'Brien's work will find this site to be a rich archive of personal stories much like those O'Brien puts forth.

The Vietnam Veteran Memorial Fund Home Page, www.vvmf.org—This organization strives to educate people about the Vietnam War by not allowing the public to forget America's recent past. This group funded the Vietnam Veterans Memorial, and their website has a great deal of relevant material for students studying O'Brien's novel, such as a virtual version of "the Wall" in Washington, D.C. Teachers will find the website's area on teaching the Vietnam War useful, as it offers guides to illuminating the Vietnam War experience in the classroom.

The Children of Vietnam Veterans Project Home Page, www.vietnamwarstudies.org—Students of O'Brien's novel will find this organization's site useful because it is about how and why Vietnam War veterans tell their families about their war experience. Beyond this, students will find descriptions of such related topics as Post Traumatic Stress Disorder and the difficulty some veterans faced when returning from the war.

Send Us Your Favorite Tips

In your quest for learning, have you ever experienced that sublime moment when you figure out a trick that saves time or trouble? Perhaps you realized that you were taking ten steps to accomplish something that could've taken two. Or, you found a little-known workaround that gets great results. If you've discovered a useful tip that helped you study more effectively and you'd like to share it, the CliffsNotes staff would love to hear from you. Go to our Web site at www.cliffsnotes.com and click the Talk to Us button. If we select your tip, we may publish it as part of CliffsNotes Daily, our exciting, free e-mail newsletter. To find out more or to subscribe to our newsletter, go to www.cliffsnotes.com on the Web.

Appendix: Map of Vietnam

Index

A

alienation, 64, 101
"Ambush," 5–60
America, Dobbins as symbol of, 17, 53
American Literature and the Experience of Vietnam (Beidler), 109
anti-war movement, 11, 97, 107
Apocalypse Now, 107
Azar
    and dancing Vietnamese girl, 61, 62
    and dead Vietnamese soldier, 57, 58
    and death of Kiowa, 70–71
    and prank on Jorgenson, 78, 80
    description of, 17

B

Backfire: A History of How American Culture Led Us into Vietnam and Made Us Fight the Way We Did (Baritz), 108
Bao Dai, 96
Baritz, Loren, 108
Beidler, Philip D., 109
Bell, Mary Anne
    character analysis, 51, 91
    description of, 18
    Rat's story of, 49–50
    struggle between darkness and light in, 100
Berdahl, Elroy, 32–33
Berlin, Paul, 5
Best American Short Stories, 6
Bowker, Norman
    and story of Kiowa's death, 63–65, 68
    character analysis, 90
    description of, 16
    feelings of alienation of, 63–64
    search for meaning by, 64–65, 68
    "The thing is," 105–106
Bright, Shining Lie, A (Sheeham), 102

C

Canada, escape to, 32–33
characters. *See also individual characters*
    connection of readers with, 23
    list of, 15–19
    symbolism of items carried by, 22
Chicago Tribune Heartland Award, 6
Children of Vietnam Veterans Project Home Page, 111
Chippering, Tom, 7
"Church," 55–56
climax, 75–76
conflicts
    between courage and fear, 34, 65
    between darkness and light, 100
    between memory and nostalgia, 65
    in O'Brien's character, 88
Conrad, Joseph, 100–101
Coppola, Francis Ford, 107
courage and fear, 34, 65
Cowling, William, 6
Crane, Stephen, 101–102
Cross, Jimmy, Lt.
    and death of Kiowa, 70
    and death of Lavender, 24
    and Martha, 22–23, 27–28
    character analysis, 89
    description of, 16
    leadership of, 89
    symbolism of items carried by, 22

D

dancing girl, symbolism of, 61–62
"The day was cloudy," 104–105
dead
    mourning for the, 46–47
    remembering the, 84–86, 93
death
    night as metaphor for, 93
    O'Brien's concepts about, 88
Delvecchio, John, 13
"Dentist, The," 46–47
detail, use of, 22, 34, 98
Diamond, Eddie, 18
Dispatches (Herr), 102

Dobbins, Henry
    and the dancing girl, 62
    and the monks, 55–56
    as symbol of America, 17, 53
    character analysis, 94
    description of, 17
    faith of, 53–54
draft
    meatpacking plant as metaphor for,
        34, 99
    O'Brien's decision about, 32–34
draft-dodging, 11
"The day was cloudy," 104–105

E

"Enemies," 38–40
escapism, 16, 85
Everything We Had (Santolini), 102

F

fact. *See* truth
faith, 53–54, 94
fear
    and courage, 34, 65
    from childhood, 47
    of soldiers, 83
fiction. *See* stories
"FieldTrip," 75, 76
fight, differences between war and a, 38
first-person narration, 28, 85
"Forty-three years old," 104–105
foreshadowing, 23
forgetting, 30
Fossie, Mark, 18, 49–50
fragmentation, of memory, 29–30
"Friends," 38–40
friendship, between soldiers, 40, 77–79
Full Metal Jacket, 107

G

genres
    Vietnam War, 10, 13, 102
    war autobiography, 68, 86
    war literature, 13, 101–102
    writer's memoir, 68
"Ghost Soldiers, The," 77–80
Gilbert, Marc Jason, 109
Going After Cacciato (O'Brien), 5, 68
"Good Form," 73

Great Esquire Fiction, 6
Greene, Graham, 13
Guggenheim Foundation, 7
guilt
    of Bowker, 65
    after Kiowa's death, 70–71
    survivor, 16, 90

H

Heart of Darkness (Conrad), 100–101
Heartland Award, 6
Hemingway, Ernest, 13, 51, 101–102
heroism, 16, 46, 64, 90
Herr, Michael, 102
Herzog, Tobey C., 109
Ho Chi Minh, 96
"How to Tell a True War Story," 42–45

I

"I know it sounds far out," 104–105
*If I Die in Combat, Box Me Up and Ship Me
    Home* (O'Brien), 5
"I'm not dead," 105–106
imagery
    night, 78, 93
    pantyhose, 53–54, 94
    star-shaped wound, 58
"In any war story," 105
"In the Field," 70, 72
In the Lake of the Woods (O'Brien), 4, 6
In Our Time (Hemingway), 51
innocence, loss of, 18, 50–51, 89, 91,
    99–100

J

James Fenimore Cooper Prize, 7
Jensen, Dave
    description of, 17
    fight between Strunk and, 38
    pact between Strunk and, 38, 40
jingoism, 11
Jorgenson, Bobby
    and O'Brien, 77–79
    description of, 18

K

Kaplan, Steven, 109
Karnow, Stanley, 109

Kathleen
    description of, 18
    lie of O'Brien to, 57, 59
    trip to Vietnam by, 75–76
Kiley, Rat
    breakdown of, 82–83
    character analysis, 92–93
    description of, 17
    "I know it sounds far out," 104–105
    letter to Lemon's sister, 42–43
    story of Mary Anne Bell, 49–50
Kiowa
    and dead Vietnamese soldier, 57–58
    and the monks, 55–56
    character analysis, 92
    death of, 15, 64–65, 68, 70–71
    description of, 16
    revisting place of death of, 75–76
Kubrick, Stanley, 107

L

lake, metaphor of the, 64–65
Lavender, Ted, 17, 24
Lemon, Curt
    character analysis, 47
    death of, 42
    description of, 16
    machoism of, 46–47
Lemon's sister, 19, 42–43
Linda
    character analysis, 93
    description of, 19
    "I'm not dead," 105–106
    O'Brien's memory of, 84–86
literary devices. *See also* narrative techniques
    foreshadowing, 23
    fragmentation, 29–30
    open words, 62
    repetition, 44
    story within a story, 85
"Lives of the Dead, The," 84–86
"Love," 27–28
love
    Linda as symbol of, 93
    link between war and, 90, 92–93
luck, role of, 71

M

magical realism, 6
"Man I Killed, The," 57–60

Martha, 19, 27–28
Massachusetts Arts and Humanities
    Foundation, 7
McCarthy, Eugene, 3, 32, 36
meaning, search for, 64–65, 75–76
meaninglessness of war, 39, 51
meatpacking plant, metaphor of, 34, 99
medium-is-the-message, 67
Melcher Award, 6
memoir, writer's, 13, 33, 68
memorials, 86
memory
    and forgetting, 30
    and writing, 88–89
    burden of, 63–65
    conflict with nostalgia, 65
    of the dead, 84–86, 93
    fragmented, 29–30
    nature of, 29–30
    theme of, 15, 23
    of Vietnam, 75–76
mental escapism, 16, 85
meta-narrative commentary, 44
metaphor
    drive around the lake, 64–65
    fight as war, 39
    Lt. Cross as war, 89
    meatpacking plant, 34, 99
    medium-is-the-message, 30
    night, 93
meta-textuality, 98
monks, 55–56
moral
    courage, 5
    uncertainty, 33

N

narrative techniques. *See also* literary devices
    free indirect discourse, 12
    non-linear presentation of events, 97
    repetition, 97
narrator
    first person, 28, 85
    third person, 28, 63, 85
National Book Award, 5
National Endowment for the Arts, 7
National Magazine Award in Fiction, 6
New York Times, The, 6
night, effects of, 78, 82–83
"Night Life," 82–83
nighttime, metaphor of, 93

North Vietnamese soldier
    description of, 18
    killing of, 57, 59
    personalization of, 58
    star-shaped wound of, 58
Northern Lights (O'Brien), 5
nostalgia and memory, 65
"Notes," 12, 67–69
Nuclear Age (O'Brien), 6

O

O'Brien, Tim (author)
    and storytelling, 4–5, 14
    awards, 5– 7
    career highlights, 4
    during Vietnam War, 3–4
    early years, 2
    education, 3–4
    effect of Vietnam War on, 4
    Going After Cacciato, 5
    *If I Die in Combat, Box Me Up and Ship
        Me Home*, 5
    In the Lake of the Woods, 4, 6
    major themes, 6
    major works, 5–7
    Northern Lights, 5
    Nuclear Age, 6
    personal life, 4
    relationship with fictional character,
        2, 10, 13, 28, 68
    "Things They Carried, The," 6
    Tomcat in Love, 7
    "The Vietnam in Me," 4, 107
    Web page of, 110
    writing style, 5, 12, 98, 99
O'Brien, Tim (fictional)
    and Jorgenson, 77–79
    character analysis, 88–89
    description of, 15–16
    draft decision of, 32–34
    "Forty-three years old," 104–105
    "In any war story," 105
    killing of soldier by, 57, 59
    persona of, 28, 43
    readjustments of, 67
    relationship with author, 10, 13, 28, 68
    return to Vietnam by, 75–76
    "The day was cloudy," 104–105
O. Henry Prize Stories, 6
"On the Rainy River," 32–33, 34–37
Orwell, George, 101–102

*Out of the Sixties: Storytelling and the Vietnam
    Generation* (Wyatt), 109
Owen, Wilfred, 13, 101–102

P

pantyhose imagery, 53–54, 94
paradoxical relationship
    between courage and fear, 34
    between death and mourning, 46–47
past, connecting present to, 30, 73, 88–89
    PBS's POV: Stories After the War Home
        Page, 110
postmodernism, 102
present, connecting past to, 30, 73, 86,
    88, 89
Prix du Meilleur Livre Etranger, 6
Pulitzer Prize, 6
Pushcart Prize, The, 6

R

randomness of war, 83
rape of Martha, 28
reader
    dialogue between author and, 88
    emotional response of, 16, 23, 30, 97
    expectations about stories of, 50
    truth of stories and, 44
religion, 55–56
remembering through storytelling, 30
repetition, 44, 97

S

Sanders, Mitchell
    and story of Mary Anne Bell, 49–50
    description of, 17
    jungle story of, 42, 44
Santolini, Al, 13, 102
setting
    nighttime, 78, 82–83
    use of detail in, 22, 34, 98
Sheeham, Neil, 102
shock, 57
Silver Star, 64
Soldier's Sweetheart, The (film), 107
soldiers
    alienation of, 101
    and monks, 55–56
    fear of, 83
    fraternity between, 40, 77–79

items carried by, 22
search for meaning by, 61–62
unstableness of, 82–83
"Speaking of Courage," 15, 63–66
"Spin," 29–31
star-shaped wound, 58
"Stockings," 53–54
story(ies)
    endings for, 50
    inability to complete a, 65
    readers' expectations about, 50
    readers' responses to, 43
    truthfulness of, 42–44, 67, 68
    understanding of, by different
        interpretive communities, 43
    war, 42, 44
    within a story, 85
storytelling
    allure and danger of, 17
    and pretending, 23
    as way of coping, 67, 68, 90
    fragmented, 29–30
    remembering through, 30
    role of, 4, 5
    theme of, 10, 15, 68
    truth in, 12, 14–15, 42, 49–50, 73, 99
stream-of-consciousness technique, 64
Strunk, Lee
    description of, 17
    fight between Jensen and, 38
    pact between Jensen and, 38, 40
"Style," 61, 62
styles, writing. *See also* narrative techniques
    magical realism, 6
    in *The Things They Carried,* 98
survivor guilt, 16, 90
"Sweetheart of Song Tra Bong," 49–52
symbolism
    of dance of Vietnamese girl, 61–62
    of eyes, 58
    in *Heart of Darkness,* 100
    of items carried by soldiers, 22
    of Linda, 93
    meta-textual, 69
    of Silver Star, 64
    of stockings, 53–54, 94
synopsis, 13–15

T

"The thing is," 105–106
themes
    allure of war, 99–100
    jingoism, 11
    memory, 15, 23
    moral courage, 5
    in O'Brien's writing, 6
    paradox between courage and fear, 34
    relationship between fact and fiction,
        50, 68
    storytelling, 10, 15, 68
    style as, 99
    time, 57–58
"Things They Carried, The," 6, 22–25
Things They Carried, The (O'Brien), 14–15
    ambiguity in, 13
    author's view of, 5
    autobiographical nature of, 10
    awards, 6
    form of, 33, 73
    genre blending in, 10, 68, 101–102
    historical context of, 96–97
    introduction to, 10
    narrative structure, 97
    reality versus fiction in, 10, 12
    style of, 98
    synopsis, 13
third-person narration, 28, 63, 85
Tim O'Brien (Herzog), 109
Tim O'Brien Web page, 110
time
    melding of past and present, 73, 86
    non-linear presentation of events, 97
    theme of, 58
Timmy, 19, 85
Tomcat in Love (O'Brien), 7
truth
    division between fiction and, 43, 68, 99
    need for emotional, 90
    personal history and, 58
    of stories, 12, 42, 49–50, 73
    types of, 73
    understanding of, by different
        interpretive communities, 43

U

Understanding Tim O'Brien (Kaplan), 109
United States, involvement in Vietnam,
    96–97

V

Veenhof, Nick, 19, 84
Vietnam, history of, 96, 97
Vietnam: A History (Karnow), 109
"Vietnam in Me, The" (O'Brien), 4, 107
Vietnam Veteran Memorial Home Page, 111
Vietnam War. *See also* war
    conflicted feelings toward, 11
    effect on Tim O'Brien, 4
    historical context of, 96, 97
    literature, 10, 13
    meaninglessness of, 39, 51, 89
    memory of, 75–76
    personalization of, 58
    political discourse on, 33
    search for meaning of, 75–76
    Tim O'Brien during, 3–4
    veterans, 13
*Vietnam War: Teaching Approaches and
    Resources* (Gilbert), 109
Vietnamese girl, dancing, 18, 61–62

W

Wade, John, 6
war. *See also* Vietnam War
    allure of, 99, 100, 101
    autobiography, 13, 33, 88
    finding meaning after, 64–65
    friendship during, 77–79
    heroes, 46
    impersonalness of, 40
    link between love and, 90, 92, 93
    literature, 13, 42, 51, 68, 86, 101–102
    loss of innocence in, 18
    memory of, 29
    randomness of, 83
    right and wrong during, 40
    role of luck in, 71
    trust during, 40
    wastefulness of, 15
water buffalo story, 42–43
Worthington, Minnesota, 2
writer's memoir, 13, 33, 68
writing
    and memory, 88–89, 93
    process of, 98
writing style, 12, 98
Wyatt, David, 109

Y

Young soldier in the field, 18

NOTES

NOTES

CliffsNotes

LITERATURE NOTES

Absalom, Absalom!
The Aeneid
Agamemnon
Alice in Wonderland
All the King's Men
All the Pretty Horses
All Quiet on the
   Western Front
All's Well &
   Merry Wives
American Poets of the
   20th Century
American Tragedy
Animal Farm
Anna Karenina
Anthem
Antony and Cleopatra
Aristotle's Ethics
As I Lay Dying
The Assistant
As You Like It
Atlas Shrugged
Autobiography of
   Ben Franklin
Autobiography of
   Malcolm X
The Awakening
Babbit
Bartleby & Benito
   Cereno
The Bean Trees
The Bear
The Bell Jar
Beloved
Beowulf
The Bible
Billy Budd & Typee
Black Boy
Black Like Me
Bleak House
Bless Me, Ultima
The Bluest Eye & Sula
Brave New World
Brothers Karamazov

The Call of the Wild &
   White Fang
Candide
The Canterbury Tales
Catch-22
Catcher in the Rye
The Chosen
The Color Purple
Comedy of Errors…
Connecticut Yankee
The Contender
The Count of
   Monte Cristo
Crime and Punishment
The Crucible
Cry, the Beloved
   Country
Cyrano de Bergerac
Daisy Miller &
   Turn…Screw
David Copperfield
Death of a Salesman
The Deerslayer
Diary of Anne Frank
Divine Comedy-I.
   Inferno
Divine Comedy-II.
   Purgatorio
Divine Comedy-III.
   Paradiso
Doctor Faustus
Dr. Jekyll and Mr. Hyde
Don Juan
Don Quixote
Dracula
Electra & Medea
Emerson's Essays
Emily Dickinson Poems
Emma
Ethan Frome
The Faerie Queene
Fahrenheit 451
Far from the Madding
   Crowd
A Farewell to Arms
Farewell to Manzanar
Fathers and Sons
Faulkner's Short Stories

Faust Pt. I & Pt. II
The Federalist
Flowers for Algernon
For Whom the Bell Tolls
The Fountainhead
Frankenstein
The French
   Lieutenant's Woman
The Giver
Glass Menagerie &
   Streetcar
Go Down, Moses
The Good Earth
The Grapes of Wrath
Great Expectations
The Great Gatsby
Greek Classics
Gulliver's Travels
Hamlet
The Handmaid's Tale
Hard Times
Heart of Darkness &
   Secret Sharer
Hemingway's
   Short Stories
Henry IV Part 1
Henry IV Part 2
Henry V
House Made of Dawn
The House of the
   Seven Gables
Huckleberry Finn
I Know Why the
   Caged Bird Sings
Ibsen's Plays I
Ibsen's Plays II
The Idiot
Idylls of the King
The Iliad
Incidents in the Life of
   a Slave Girl
Inherit the Wind
Invisible Man
Ivanhoe
Jane Eyre
Joseph Andrews
The Joy Luck Club
Jude the Obscure

Julius Caesar
The Jungle
Kafka's Short Stories
Keats & Shelley
The Killer Angels
King Lear
The Kitchen God's Wife
The Last of the
   Mohicans
Le Morte d'Arthur
Leaves of Grass
Les Miserables
A Lesson Before Dying
Light in August
The Light in the Forest
Lord Jim
Lord of the Flies
The Lord of the Rings
Lost Horizon
Lysistrata & Other
   Comedies
Macbeth
Madame Bovary
Main Street
The Mayor of
   Casterbridge
Measure for Measure
The Merchant
   of Venice
Middlemarch
A Midsummer Night's
   Dream
The Mill on the Floss
Moby-Dick
Moll Flanders
Mrs. Dalloway
Much Ado About
   Nothing
My Ántonia
Mythology
Narr. …Frederick
   Douglass
Native Son
New Testament
Night
1984
Notes from the
   Underground

The Odyssey
Oedipus Trilogy
Of Human Bondage
Of Mice and Men
The Old Man and
   the Sea
Old Testament
Oliver Twist
The Once and
   Future King
One Day in the Life of
   Ivan Denisovich
One Flew Over the
   Cuckoo's Nest
100 Years of Solitude
O'Neill's Plays
Othello
Our Town
The Outsiders
The Ox Bow Incident
Paradise Lost
A Passage to India
The Pearl
The Pickwick Papers
The Picture of
   Dorian Gray
Pilgrim's Progress
The Plague
Plato's Euthyphro...
Plato's The Republic
Poe's Short Stories
A Portrait of the
   Artist...
The Portrait of a Lady
The Power and
   the Glory
Pride and Prejudice
The Prince
The Prince and
   the Pauper
A Raisin in the Sun
The Red Badge of
   Courage
The Red Pony
The Return of the
   Native
Richard II
Richard III

The Rise of
   Silas Lapham
Robinson Crusoe
Roman Classics
Romeo and Juliet
The Scarlet Letter
A Separate Peace
Shakespeare's
   Comedies
Shakespeare's Histories
Shakespeare's
   Minor Plays
Shakespeare's Sonnets
Shakespeare's Tragedies
Shaw's Pygmalion &
   Arms...
Silas Marner
Sir Gawain...Green
   Knight
Sister Carrie
Slaughterhouse-Five
Snow Falling on Cedars
Song of Solomon
Sons and Lovers
The Sound and the Fury
Steppenwolf &
   Siddhartha
The Stranger
The Sun Also Rises
T.S. Eliot's Poems &
   Plays
A Tale of Two Cities
The Taming of the
   Shrew
Tartuffe, Misanthrope...
The Tempest
Tender Is the Night
Tess of the D'Urbervilles
Their Eyes Were
   Watching God
Things Fall Apart
The Three Musketeers
To Kill a Mockingbird
Tom Jones
Tom Sawyer
Treasure Island &
   Kidnapped
The Trial

Tristram Shandy
Troilus and Cressida
Twelfth Night
Ulysses
Uncle Tom's Cabin
The Unvanquished
Utopia
Vanity Fair
Vonnegut's Works
Waiting for Godot
Walden
Walden Two
War and Peace
Who's Afraid of
   Virginia...
Winesburg, Ohio
The Winter's Tale
The Woman Warrior
Worldly Philosophers
Wuthering Heights
A Yellow Raft in
   Blue Water

Check Out the All-New CliffsNotes Guides

TECHNOLOGY TOPICS

Balancing Your Check-
   book with Quicken
Buying and Selling
   on eBay™
Buying Your First PC
Creating a Winning
   PowerPoint 2000
   Presentation
Creating Web Pages
   with HTML
Creating Your First
   Web Page
Exploring the World
   with Yahoo!
Getting on the Internet
Going Online with AOL
Making Windows 98
   Work for You
Setting Up a
   Windows 98
   Home Network
Shopping Online Safely
Upgrading and
   Repairing Your PC
Using Your First iMac™
Using Your First PC
Writing Your First
   Computer Program

PERSONAL FINANCE TOPICS

Budgeting & Saving
   Your Money
Getting a Loan
Getting Out of Debt
Investing for the
   First Time
Investing in
   401(k) Plans
Investing in IRAs
Investing in
   Mutual Funds
Investing in the
   Stock Market
Managing Your Money
Planning Your
   Retirement
Understanding
   Health Insurance
Understanding
   Life Insurance

CAREER TOPICS

Delivering a Winning
   Job Interview
Finding a Job
   on the Web
Getting a Job
Writing a Great Resume

A Giordano y a todos sus amigos

Título original: **É una parola**

Colección **libros para soñar**®

© del texto y de las ilustraciones: Arianna Papini, 2012
© de la traducción: Lola Barceló, 2013
© de esta edición: Kalandraka Ediciones Andalucía, 2013
Avión Cuatro Vientos, 7. 41013 Sevilla
Telefax: 954 095 558
andalucia@kalandraka.com
www.kalandraka.com

Impreso en Gráficas Anduriña, Poio
Primera edición: marzo, 2013
ISBN: 978-84-92608-71-3
DL: SE 254-2013
Reservados todos los derechos

53310677 04/14

SER AMIGOS

ARIANNA PAPINI

kalandraka

SER AMIGOS ES...

SENTIRSE IGUALES
AUNQUE SEAMOS DIFERENTES

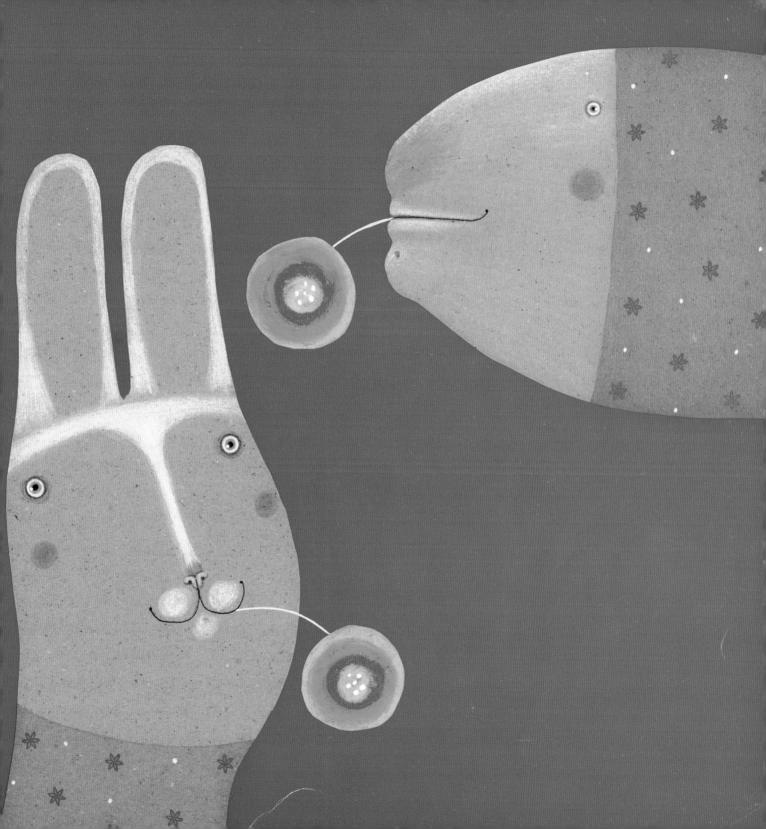

NO DAR IMPORTANCIA
A NUESTRO ASPECTO

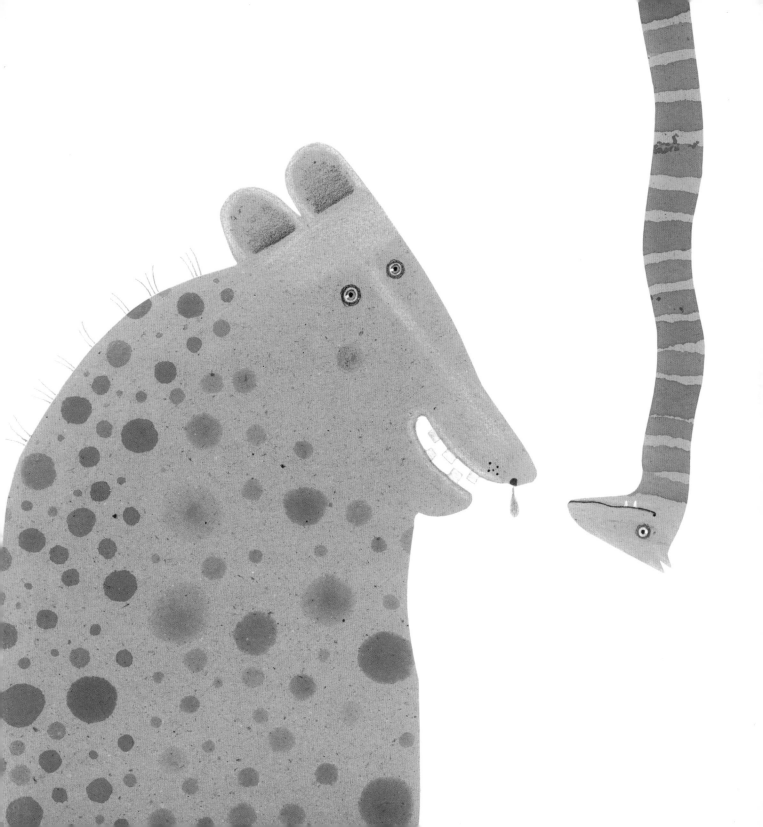

APOYARSE
EN LOS TIEMPOS DIFÍCILES

DESEAR QUE LOS BUENOS MOMENTOS
NO SE ACABEN NUNCA

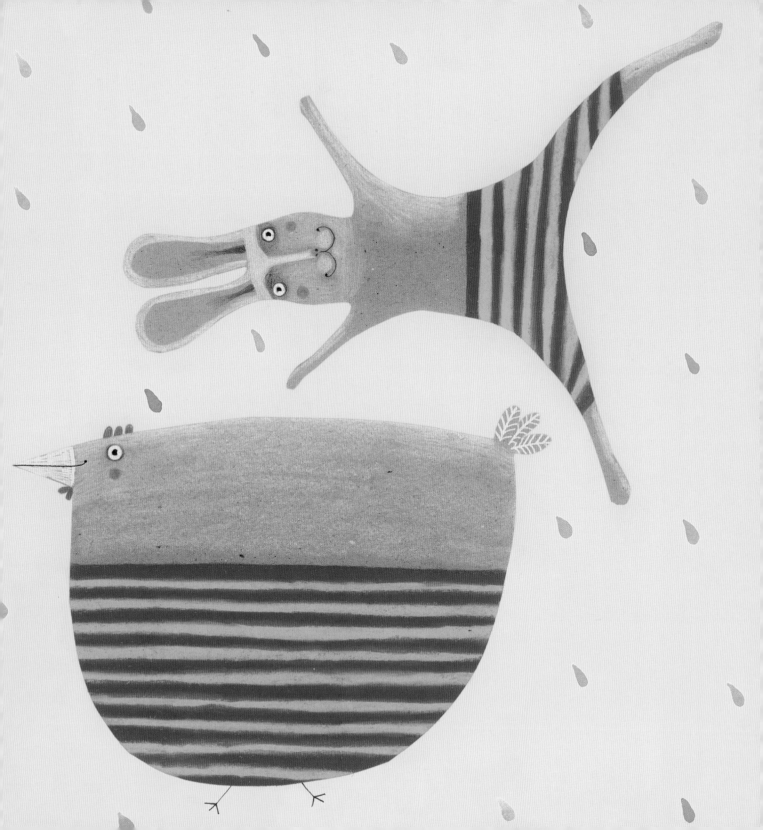

AYUDARSE
EL UNO AL OTRO

CONTARSE SECRETOS

SABER QUE SIEMPRE HAY ALGUIEN CERCA,
INCLUSO CUANDO MENOS TE LO ESPERAS

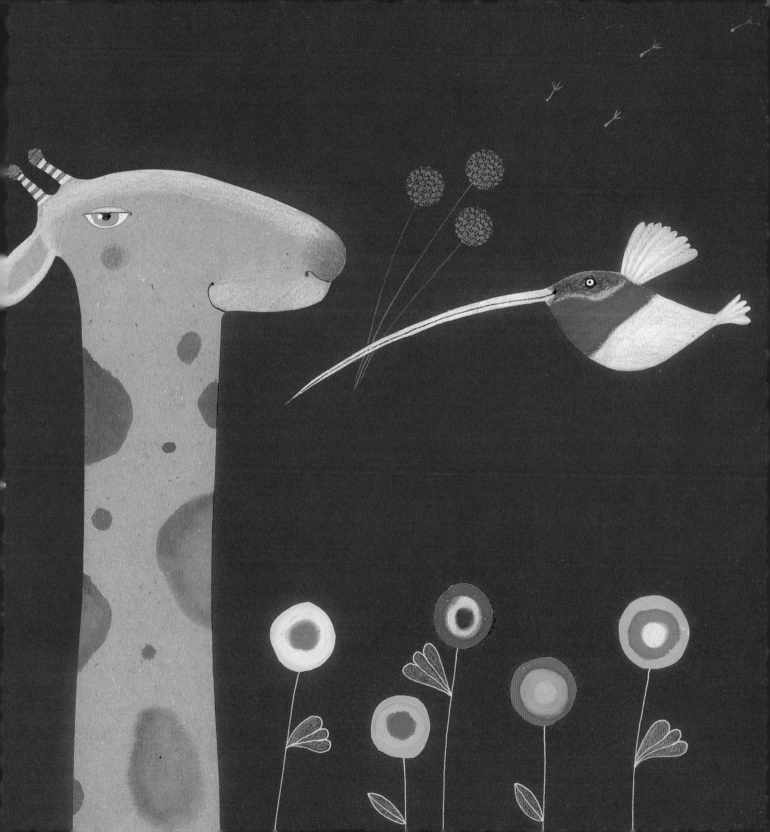

DIVERTIRSE JUNTOS

CONFIAR
EN EL OTRO

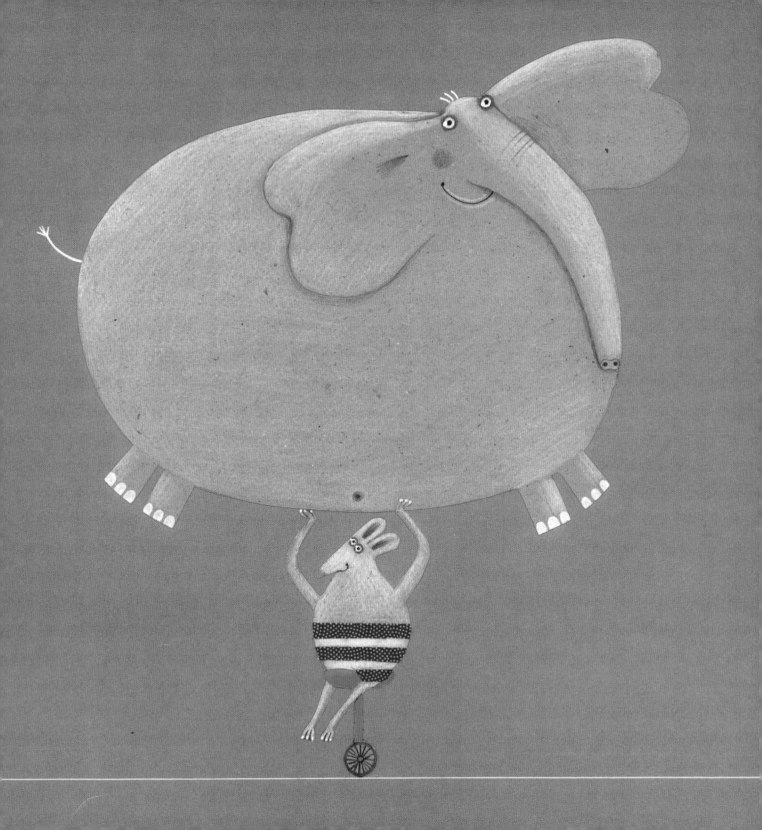

SOÑAR
EL MISMO SUEÑO

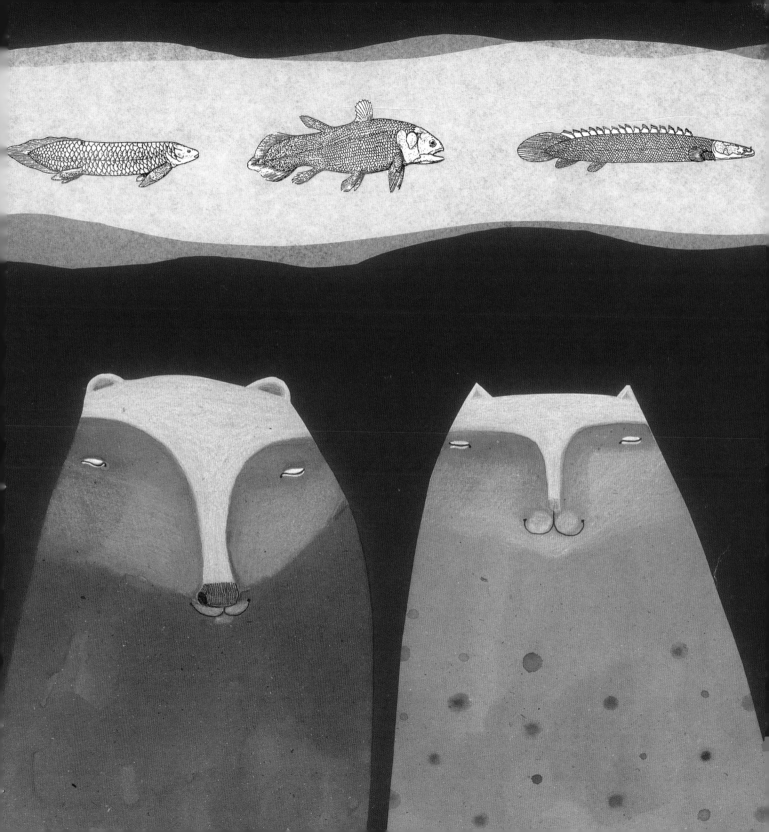

COMPARTIR
UN LUGAR ESPECIAL

DARSE CARIÑO

¡ESO ES SER AMIGOS!